CULTURE CHANGE

CRACKING THE CULTURE CODE

KEVIN
BROWNSEY

R^ethink

First published in Great Britain in 2023
by Rethink Press
(www.rethinkpress.com)

This book is dedicated to those leaders I have worked with who suspended their personal preferences and pursued the culture their organisations needed to be successful.

27/12/22

٢٢/١٢/٢٢

Contents

Introduction

C racking the Culture Code is my attempt to capture ten years of culture work in a reference manual for managers and leaders who want to understand and change their culture. Each chapter is focused on a specific element of culture change, but many of the ideas in this book are co-dependent. It's amazing, and a bit sobering, to realise that ten years' work can be summarised in a 240-page book.

My experiences and insights are based on thousands of data points, hundreds of hours of dialogue and ten years of hands-on experience, plus more than my fair share of failure. The failures were my most valuable experiences. I'll try to share these with humour and honesty and I'll use real, but anonymised, examples wherever possible. I'll also be honest about some change processes I ran that simply didn't work and attempt to explain the learning gained. Five days into writing this book, I ditched the working title *Culture: The Chaos and the Clarity* and replaced it with *Cracking the Culture Code: Leading Successful Culture Change.* The way the chapters were unfolding and the emphasis I was placing on the good, the bad, and the sometimes unforgiveable ways in which leaders choose to handle the topic of culture change was dominating my content. It dawned on me that the real purpose of my book was to provide some simple solutions and frameworks to help leaders avoid the mistakes so many make when embarking on culture change. Culture change is the most important work you will ever do. Please don't be a part-time leader of culture change. Don't be that leader who talks about behaviour change but never changes their own; who evangelises about treating people as human beings, but treats them disrespectfully when the pressure for results is on; who loses patience with the employee who is trying to change but temporarily lacks the skill; or who treats culture change as a 'project' with fixed milestones.

This particular story begins in July 2008 when I uprooted my family from a sleepy North Yorkshire village and relocated to Warsaw, Poland. I'd been appointed Commercial Director for a global brewing company and was looking forward to an exciting period as an ex-pat executive with all the privileges that brings. The job was big and demanding, but not particularly inspiring. Ways of working in Poland were not as advanced as I had been used to. There seemed to be a national trait of resistance when I, or we (ex-pats), tried to change anything. Stony silence met every proposal for change or request for feedback and people nodded or sometimes uttered agreement to other requests that rarely seemed to actually get actioned. No one seemed the slightest bit interested in others' roles, and no one ever challenged a peer, let alone me (at least not publicly). When I tried to empower team members, they simply complained (to each other) that I was asking them to do my job for me. I was struggling to communicate. I was struggling, full stop.

Slowly, I made a few friends and built a little trust. Things started to improve, but there was still this apparent reluctance to take added responsibility and a complete absence of challenge of each other. There was a block – but why? It took me several months to realise that all of these shared behaviours could be explained by cultural beliefs. I was judging my team rather than seeking to understand them. I had arrived in another country with my paradigm of right and wrong, my definition of 'normal', ready to impart my (superior) knowledge. Lucky them. I hoped to assimilate a technically competent and successful group of leaders into my way of thinking, my way of being. I was wrong to try, and even more wrong to judge them. At this point I became fascinated by the topic of organisational culture: how it enables or disables effective working, and how difficult it appeared to be to change.

Since 2012 I have dedicated my professional life to understanding organisational culture, helping leaders change their culture and adding to the debate on this most important of organisational topics. I have been brutal in my criticism of commentators who treat culture as a superficial buzzword and of leaders who don't see it as a strategic imperative. I have championed the leaders who are able to suspend personal preference to pursue what their organisation actually needs (see Chapter 5: Take Off Your Glasses) and are brave enough to recognise their own role in creating dysfunctional environments.

The design of the book follows a simple structure that I have adopted in my consulting work. The first few chapters look at the topics associated with preparing for culture change, followed by a series of chapters looking at implementing culture change. In each chapter I propose some conceptual content and real-life reflection, followed by some suggested dialogues for you to simulate with your team. Dialogue, after all, is probably the most important skill required for a diverse group of people to align on an organisational belief system. Each time you see the dialogue symbol, you may wish to put the book down, think about the question(s) posed and then discuss with your team before moving on in the book. This way, you will take your team on a dialogue journey. The first couple of dialogues will help you reflect on your team's attitude to culture. If you have an appetite to continue reading beyond this point, further dialogues will be focused on preparing for change and in-change challenges.

The preparation for culture change needs to be thorough. There's a lot to do and discuss before you even begin to address the change agenda. Leaders who do this part well learn to be curious again (Chapter 1: I Wonder…). They ensure their intuition is supported by data (Chapter 3: Data, Data, Data) and above all, they ensure a psychologically safe environment exists before throwing change and uncertainty at their people (Chapter 7: Safe Is Not Soft). Critically, leaders of culture change recognise that they, too, must be willing to be vulnerable, be open to change and be both resilient and transparent when they are facing up to their personal consequences (Chapter 8: Consequences).

Once the preparation is done, the implementation begins. Here, I have expressed at length my advocacy of tight/loose approaches (Chapter 10: Tight/Loose) and energy flow (Chapter 13: Energy Flow). I have found a new ability to be patient with those that really try and do something constructive within their organisation, and even more supportive of those that place themselves in a deliberately vulnerable place. I'm not so patient with the part-time leaders (Chapter 9: Part-time Leader) and the pseudo-experts (Chapter 14: Pseudo-experts) who confidently announce culture change and then move on to the next sexy project on their lists. We wouldn't 'announce' completion of strategy, so why do we think we can announce the completion of culture change (Chapter 11: Abracadabra)?

In writing this book, I am indebted to Geert Hofstede.[1] In the 1980s, Hofstede conducted research exploring how we can structure cultural beliefs into understandable dimensions, and how we can apply these dimensions to the workplace in various countries (see

---

1   G Hofstede, *Cultures and Organisations: Software of the mind, Third Edition* (McGraw-Hill Education, 2010)

Chapter 3: Data, Data, Data). Hofstede defined one of his cultural dimensions as Masculine vs Feminine. I'd like to stress at the outset that 'masculine' and 'feminine' is used in this context as a culture label, not a gender label. There are several references in this book to the concept of masculine and feminine cultural characteristics and consequences. Twenty-two years into the third millennium, it is clear to me that it is this aspect of culture which will need the most active attention in organisations that wish to be successful in the future. There are also several references to national culture types which emanate from Hofstede's work.

The truth is, companies and organisations are successful the world over and there are many different culture types enabling that success. There is no one formula for perfect culture, despite what we read in the myriad of books emerging from mainly North America. Culture is diverse and unique to individual businesses, and once we recognise this one small point, we can start to create the environment that works for us rather than the stereotype advocated by well-intentioned gurus. I am not a guru, and I won't be recommending a culture 'type' to fix all your problems. While writing this book I experienced a few of my own real-time 'aha' moments, which I have recognised and revealed in my writing. We are all learning, and it is not my intention to pretend I have all the answers. Instead, I will be advocating a thought and dialogue process to help you get to your required outcome. Well, actually, your required belief system. In the past ten years, 'culture change' is probably, and sadly, the greatest leadership failure of all. This book is my small contribution to ensuring the next ten years will be different.

DIALOGUE

Purpose: For you to gain a fundamental understanding of how your team views culture in the context of it being an *input* to success or an *outcome* of success.

Facilitate a discussion by asking this question: Does culture drive performance or does performance drive culture? If you only hear voices on one side of the debate, then play devil's advocate to stimulate some controversy. Answering this question may explain why culture doesn't change in your organisation.

With reference to the table below, which of these comments emerged in your conversation?

When Culture is a driver of performance...	When Culture is an outcome of success...
'Our culture defines what we believe, how we behave and the way we work together.'	'If we're successful, people will be more engaged and the culture will be positive.'
'The most critical element of organisational growth is learning and innovation.'	'The most critical element of organisational growth is execution.'
'The most important role of managers is to develop the capability of their team.'	'The most important role of managers is to supervise successful task completion.'

If your team sees positive culture as a welcome outcome of success, you are probably working in a team or organisation that focuses mainly on the metrics of strategic execution, and for whom results in the short term are important. People who get the best results get promoted, often irrespective of how they get them. There will be constant pressure to perform and one's worth is measured by one's bonus. You may recognise leaders of these organisations in many of the examples provided in this book.

If your team sees culture as a driver of performance, you are probably working with a team that focuses mainly on people and culture, and for whom employee engagement, learning and long-term indicators of success are important. People get promoted according to their ability to lead and handle complexity in the long term. One's worth is measured by one's positive impact on others and one's followership. This book is designed to help you become a leader of one of these teams or organisations.

PART ONE

PREPARING FOR CULTURE CHANGE

As leaders, it's our obligation to be curious and wonder. It is a myth that people expect us to 'know' everything.

1

I Wonder...

In the words of Sixto Rodriguez, 'I wonder...'

'I wonder what would happen if we...'

'I wonder if we could improve the way we...'

'I wonder how they...'

'I wonder what a woman would say...'

'I wonder what a man would say...'

Curiosity seems to work in contradiction to the majority of life skills, which mostly develop and mature over time. We're born with curiosity in abundance and then it gradually gets lost. As kids, we ask constant questions (sometimes to the annoyance of our parents) and we explore and enquire without fear of judgement. When we're young, it appears our appetite for knowledge, learning and growth is insatiable. Then life experience kicks in, we become 'normalised', we start to believe we have the answers (or *should* have the answers) and our learning slows down. Education systems that are focused on finding the 'solution' to a problem or *the* answer don't help. Once solved, those answers are banked, rarely (if ever) to be challenged again. As we grow up and the influences on our thinking become ever more complex, human beings tend to retreat back to what they know from their own experience rather than open themselves up to other people's truths and life experiences. Truths that may challenge our own 'truths' and threaten our authority and security are ignored. The adage, 'I know what I like and I like what I know,' prevails.

In day-to-day leadership roles, there is pressure to have the answers, and the more senior the role, the more certain you are expected to be. Where does this expectation come from? Others? Ourselves? Company culture certainly determines our attitude to leadership. For example, most Anglo-American company cultures are 'masculine': winning is everything, confidence is expected, knowing the answer is important and making decisions assertively and firmly is viewed as a leadership strength. In more 'feminine' business cultures (often found in Scandinavian companies), leadership is consultative and an aligned answer is more important than a quick, decisive answer. Modesty is expected and care for people is usually valued more than winning. (I would like to stress again that this is *feminine company culture* I am referring to, not the impact of female gender on culture.) A feminine culture is supportive, caring, empathic and collaborative. A masculine culture will be target- and results-oriented, assertive and competitive.

Note: The terms masculine/competitive and the terms feminine/ consultative are used interchangeably from here onwards.

The cultural dimension of feminine vs masculine and the female/ male gender balance in your leadership team are *not* directly linked. As an example, a Swedish all-male management board will be significantly more culturally 'feminine' than an all-female UK or US management board. As an aside, this is also why some of the expected and assumed outcomes of driving gender balance may not always be forthcoming (see Chapter 17: The Feminine Touch).

Finding the balance

To masculine/competitive types, consultative types may be slow and seek to avoid accountability. To feminine/consultative types, competitive types can be superficial and shoot from the hip, without regard for consequence. The irony is competitive cultures often talk the talk of consultation and care, but rarely adapt their behaviour to this declaration. Similarly, consultative cultures know they could be more results-oriented, but sometimes struggle to take the steps to be so.

I experienced this phenomenon first-hand when working on culture change with a Scandinavian client. I asked if I could attend a few internal meetings to gain a feel for the business. I'd already run a culture diagnostic which indicated a strongly feminine (in a cultural sense) business and agreed to attend a quarterly review session at their regional head office in Warsaw, Poland. The agenda looked quite standard: a review of quarterly results, feedback on the recent employee engagement survey and a look ahead to the next quarter. What wasn't standard was the time allocated to each session. The review of results took about ten minutes. The CEO presented disappointing numbers for the quarter, but he recognised that everyone was 'trying hard' and he was convinced he had the team to 'turn the year around'. He highlighted a couple of teams who had cooperated 'beautifully' on a product launch and thanked one of his fellow board members for helping him with his own personal development. He then handed over to one of his team for the employee engagement results. At this point, I thought the whole session would last about thirty minutes and I was preparing a couple of questions for the Q&A. I didn't expect what happened next. The energy in the room had changed. It was more charged. People looked alive and they were whispering with almost childish excitement. The employee engagement results were good and the presenter made sure he recognised the progress in every team. If there was no progress then he recognised the effort people had made. The session lasted over an hour. There were lots of questions and references about how happy and appreciative people were with some recent wellbeing changes the management team had made. The biggest cheer of the day was heard when the overall 'happiest team' award was made to a leader in logistics, and he received his recognition in a way I can only liken to the way a stage performer receives the applause of an adoring audience. He was the hero of the day, the manager to aspire to and emulate. I was speechless. I'd never seen such acknowledgement of employee engagement and such a lack of apparent concern for poor results. In the companies I'd worked for, 'employee engagement' wouldn't have even appeared on the agenda with business results this bad, but in a culture so skewed towards care, empathy and support, this was normal. This organisational culture was strong, but imbalanced. Over the next ten years, I worked with the 'emerging talent' group in this same company, placing an emphasis on cultural self-awareness and opening their eyes to alternative ways of thinking. Gradually, I sensed a more balanced approach, not only through my influence, but also because the host country personnel in Poland became more senior within the organisation and the ways of working became a bit more 'competitive' (culturally Poland is a masculine country). In this example, the respect for people allowed genuine curiosity to thrive within the organisation. Gaining this balance is much harder in competitive worlds where the degree of curiosity for exploring differences is much lower, so the strong emphasis on 'results first, people second' is harder to influence.

I have had significantly more success as a consultant in helping culturally feminine companies become more masculine than I have helping culturally masculine companies become more feminine. I wonder if this is because I'm a man, or because masculine cultures are less adaptable and open to influence than feminine ones? I suggest the latter is more likely as my business partners, all women, have had exactly the same experience (see Chapter 17: The Feminine Touch).

To varying degrees, we are all restricted and constricted by the culture we are born into. If we operate in a competitive culture and compound this competitiveness with hierarchical ways of working, we see even more pressure on leaders to 'know'. Hierarchical leaders are expected to make decisions, take responsibility and lead, for goodness' sake!

The skill is to know what you are, and *why* you are what you are. Only through gaining self-awareness can we establish whether enquiry and consultation are under- or over-played. If we only ask for feedback from those like us, our paradigms will be reinforced and our beliefs further entrenched. We need to understand alternative beliefs from alternative cultures if we want to see things more holistically. The answer lies in finding a balance, but in my experience, the cultural dimension of feminine vs masculine (or consultative vs competitive) is the least likely to change significantly.

A reduction in curiosity as we grow older and a requirement in most cultures to have the answer and be an all-knowing, 'oracle' leader can make leadership lonely and isolating. It may also become short-term as we increasingly apply previous solutions to current problems. This means we probably don't consider different options, experiment, learn or grow.

My work with clients has taken me to different countries and different continents. The constant in most organisations is a distinct lack of curiosity – even in those organisations that have it labelled as a 'core competence'. Leaders know that learning is critical, and curiosity drives learning, so why is curiosity such a rare characteristic and such a common statement of intent? The reason for some leaders is that 'curiosity' is too often what I describe as a *projected competence*. Projected competencies emerge often during culture change and are defined in our work as the competencies a leader needs to see more of in others, but doesn't need (or doesn't see the need) to change in themselves. Of course, this isn't stated or sometimes even conscious, but often emerges as the reality. Do you have blind-spot projected competencies? How do you know?

Curiosity in action

Imagine two experts in a room, enquiring about each other's separate, but related, work. This is when synergy happens. Two respectful, co-dependent people enquiring how they may be able to help each other. A couple of years ago, I was facilitating a discussion between a group of people working on innovation projects in a consumer goods business in the UK. Their biggest issue was constantly shortening timeframes to launch new products. They simply couldn't deliver a quality, well-researched and tested product within the time allocated. Their boss was pushing hard, looking for ways to speed up the process, but it wasn't happening. Too many failed launches were creating huge tension in the business.

From a cultural perspective, the key is to know what you are, and why you are what you are.

I asked where the pressure for faster product launches was coming from. The response was that the commercial director was telling the CEO the only way to hit sales targets was to get new product development (NPD) to market quicker. The CEO subsequently put pressure on the marketing director to speed up innovation, and the pressure landed on the innovation team. A great example of a lack of empathy, driven by a lack of understanding caused by a lack of curiosity. Basically, all NPD projects were being rushed, launched badly and underperforming. The innovation team's reputation was in tatters and confidence low. I sensed the solution, or at least part of it, was for the leaders of commercial and marketing to put their heads together and try to build a better understanding of each other's pressures. I gave them instructions to ask two identical questions of each other:

1. How could I help you deliver your objectives?

2. What's the biggest issue your team has with my team?

They had started the process of enquiry. Within five days, they would stop one of four innovation projects, place more resource on the favoured three and push out launch dates slightly. Critically, both functional leaders became more confident about success due to the detailed and creative launch plans developed by a mixed team of specialists. They confidently stretched the forecasts to over-compensate for the time and product compromises. Two of the three products were actually launched early and beat forecast. The third was a little late, but on target. A great result which has resulted in a new way of planning product launches, an extended timeline for NPD that allows for some experimentation and failure, and cross-functional teams much more confident with their forecasts due to a high-quality and integrated planning process. More importantly, a more engaged innovation team, higher in confidence, with a growing reputation for excellence. Everyone wins.

DIALOGUE

Purpose: To practise becoming curious again (a basic pre-condition of culture change).

Think of someone who you work closely with, but whose role you don't fully understand and whom you suspect may not fully understand yours. Have lunch together and ask them these two questions:

1. How could I help you deliver your objectives?

2. What's the biggest issue your team has with my team?

Once your colleague recovers from the shock, I promise you, it will be a lunch well spent.

Self-reflection

Ask yourself these questions. Which answers are you least satisfied with? Ask each member of your team the same questions over the next week or two:

- Do I allow ideas to be fully explored, or do I sometimes close down discussions too early?

- Do I learn from my colleagues, or do I show a lack of interest in their work and their challenges?

- Do I respect the expertise of others, or do I sometimes allow my opinion to override theirs?

- Do I really understand issues fully, or do I look at some problems at a superficial level only?

- Do I have the courage to raise sensitive issues, or do I back down from asking questions that could cause waves?

Our beliefs drive
our behaviours,
and our behaviours
drive our outcomes.

2

The 'Culture' Word

The word 'culture' has different meaning to different people(s). For some, it's a concept of 'being' based on a set of values and beliefs. Others try a more philosophical approach, using sentences like, 'Our culture is defined by the behaviour we tolerate.' Maybe, but if we define culture by the behaviour we tolerate, most people start to think of negative behaviours that *shouldn't* be tolerated. Do we really want to define our culture by the worst examples of the behaviour we observe? Nobody wants bad behaviour in their organisation, and we shouldn't tolerate it, but culture should be seen as a positive enabler of business activity rather than an ambition to be the *least bad* group of people we can be. This only serves to help employees understand *what not to be*, rather than what they need to be, or can be. Some organisations refer to culture as the 'glue that binds us together'. This gives the topic of culture a vague intangibility. The danger is that we start to confuse organisational 'purpose' with cultural soundbites. Our statement of *purpose* is what *binds us together*. Our *culture* is a more complex nut to crack. It helps us understand 'how' we pursue this purpose successfully. For these reasons, I'm not a fan of philosophical definitions of culture – nor definitions that only take us to the avoidance of the bad stuff (see Chapter 7: Safe Is Not Soft).

For others still, culture may be described as an outcome, for example, 'performance culture' or 'innovation culture'. These outcome-type descriptions can be seductive to leaders, especially charismatic or superficial leaders who deal in soundbites, but dangerous and often confusing for employees. Let's take the old classic: 'winning culture'. How many organisations do you know that don't want to win? None, right? We know the aim is to be successful, but all we've done to our employees by announcing a 'winning culture' is placed pressure on them. The consequence of words like 'winning' is that losing or failing become unacceptable, so they avoid it. They don't take risks and stop experimenting. When something goes wrong, you can be sure that someone else will be blamed. Nothing is learned.

Rather than dwell on what it's *not* and phrases which have little meaning, I'd like to explore the word in a way that assists us to do something to help the business in a positive sense. To do this, I will refer to a 'beliefs/behaviour/outcomes' model, where our beliefs drive our behaviours, and our behaviours drive our outcomes.

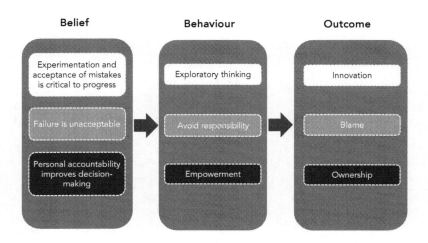

Belief/Behaviour/Outcome Model

Start with beliefs

Ten years in the culture world has taught me that successful culture change *always* starts with an understanding of the beliefs that prevail in the organisation. If we believe that 'experimentation and learning from mistakes is a critical part of driving improvement', we will encourage behaviours such as exploratory thinking, problem analysis and empowered decision-making. This, in turn, may eventually result in an outcome of innovation or learning. If we hold a belief that we should avoid mistakes and get things right the first time, every time, then we may observe behaviours such as avoiding risks and hiding mistakes. This will result in making problems so invisible that they never get raised, let alone solved, or the blaming of others when mistakes are revealed.

A difference in belief about something as simple as making a mistake can take us to different outcomes. The leaders who advocate 'right first time, every time' do not do this to create a blame culture. They are aspiring to high standards and high-quality work, but the consequence of well-intended headlines can often have the opposite effect when translated through the beliefs/behaviour/outcome model.

In the past ten years, I have asked leaders to describe their organisational culture on several hundred occasions and their responses are as diverse as their personalities. Leaders rarely have any trouble responding to the request, and nearly all reply with authority and certainty in their voice. This is often where the problems start. Virtually every leader I have spoken to understands the question, answers with conviction and sticks resolutely to his or her perspective when challenged. Putting it simply, every leader is an expert on culture, and typically, a leader's views on culture are usually quite fixed. This is either a topic so important, or so current and fashionable, that leaders feel they *should* hold a strong opinion, or they genuinely *do* hold a strong opinion. Whichever it is, we usually start a culture change process with seven or eight senior people expressing strongly held opinions, constantly repeating the same mantras just in case we didn't hear them the first twenty or thirty times. If we're lucky, these seven or eight senior people will fall into two or three loosely aligned clusters, but often this is not the case. Even where a set of organisational values exists, apparently underpinning a definition of organisational culture, we still see and hear vastly different interpretations of these values. Even when the high-level belief is aligned by the same words, it may not be aligned by the same *meaning*, and translates into different behaviours. If the organisation spans different countries and regions, the complexity increases considerably. It is easy to see why the topic of culture is thrown in the bin and labelled 'too difficult'.

I'm currently working with a French organisation. They have an ambition to empower and trust the leaders below the management board more. However, one of the French board members caveated this recently by saying, 'Unless they make the wrong decision, and then I may have to step in and change it.' He is working in a hierarchy and he can't let go of it. On hearing this particular comment, another board member responded by saying, 'That defeats the object and disrespects our leaders.' Two vastly different interpretations of the same intent held by leaders in adjacent offices. The issue is that the *belief* is different for each of them. For the former, it's something like, 'We should only empower people to make the right decisions.' For the latter, it's more like, 'Our people should be empowered to do their jobs and learn from their mistakes.' To avoid confusing their employees, these two leaders need to agree on an aligned belief for empowerment.

When a team, or more usually a CEO aided and abetted by a progressive HR leader, decides the topic of culture has become too important to ignore, the process of culture change may begin. Culture change is less of a process and more an evolving, and involving, dialogue – up, down and across the organisation: a complex web of planned and spontaneous conversations that gradually change the language, the behaviours and the ways of working that prevail. Using a culture model such as the one explained in Chapter 4 (Culture Enables Strategy) helps leaders align on language and meaning. This evolving process is sometimes so subtle that we have to remind teams where they started, for them to appreciate where they are.

 DIALOGUE

Purpose: To become familiar with the basic 'beliefs drive behaviours, and behaviours drive outcomes' model of culture change.

Ask your team to discuss what, if any, cultural beliefs are shared by the group. A team that struggles with this discussion probably isn't creating any sort of consistent culture. A team that manages to agree on two or three core beliefs can subsequently discuss the consequential behaviours emerging from these beliefs and the outcomes they drive. We often observe a lightbulb moment when leaders realise the outcomes of their beliefs are far removed from their intentions. They start to understand the linkages between beliefs, behaviours and outcomes and their personal and collective impact on the organisational culture. The result of this discussion is often a recognition that they need to redefine a set of shared beliefs to drive the behaviours and outcomes that will enable their strategic execution. Please note the word 'shared'. Culture is shared by definition. No single leader can create a culture by themselves (see Chapter 12: Everyone, Or No One).

For many leaders, behaviours become the main area of focus, and yet for others, it's the working practices or the 'way we do things' around here. In reality, it is, of course, both. Contrary to popular belief, the *way we do things* around here is not so intangible. This is our processes and practices, in other words 'our ways of working'. We will explore the critical alignment of behaviours and ways of working in Chapter 6 (Yin And Yang).

Once we've had the first discussion about culture and realised (almost certainly) that the leadership group need to find greater consistency about how beliefs and required culture are articulated and communicated within the organisation, we can use a diagnostic tool to understand the detail. The first critical step in understanding our culture is getting aligned on what we mean by it and being prepared to suspend thirty to forty years of assumptions and paradigms about what is right and wrong. This is not easy, and sadly, far too many leaders are not prepared to do this. This is especially true in cultures where leaders are supposed to be strong, decisive people holding the answers to all possible questions. This is precisely where my attempt to empower my team in 2008 went wrong. I thought I was being progressive and helping them develop. They thought I should complete certain tasks myself as it defined my role as a leader. My failure to see this subtle difference in perspective led to me judging them as incompetent and expressing frustration. Instead, I should have asked them what they believed the role of a leader was and explained my perspective before finding a way forward. I assumed they wanted the same egalitarian environment that my UK teams had desired. Truth is, they did want something similar, but by finding common understanding rather than by imposition.

We all grow up learning right and wrong from the key people in our lives: parents, grandparents, carers, teachers, siblings, coaches and friends. We take those lifelong beliefs into the workplace and

It is consistently the case that feminine cultures are more open to change than masculine cultures.

then someone comes along and says, 'Why do you think this way?' This rocks our boat of stability. The ability of leaders to suspend long-held beliefs and listen to the beliefs of others is the critical first step to what I call 'belief alignment', which is the foundation of culture change (see Chapter 5: Take Off Your Glasses).

 DIALOGUE

Purpose: To strip back behaviours to the beliefs that drive them and understand how different your colleagues' beliefs may be.

Select two or three required leadership behaviours and ask your discussion group to each write down what they believe underpins the need for these behaviours in your organisation on separate cards. (You are not asking them to define the behaviour, you are asking them *why* the behaviour is needed. For example, if 'collaboration' is the required behaviour, ask the group, 'Why do we need to collaborate?')

Ask the group to exchange cards. Each individual then reads the 'belief' on the card handed to them and tries to explain the meaning. This is an excellent way to step into each other's shoes, build empathy and see different perspectives. Possible beliefs underpinning collaboration include:

- By working cross-functionally, we will devise better solutions.

- You will always accomplish more with the help of others than you will ever accomplish alone.

- If I find people who I like working with, I will enjoy going to work each day.

- There are times when collaborating is the right thing to do, and times when it's not.

Self-reflection

- How often do I align my interpretation of organisational culture with my colleagues'?

- When did I last *steal with pride* from someone else's perspective of culture?

- Do I describe culture in terms of outcomes or beliefs?

- Do I use a language that is easily understood when advocating changes in behaviour?

The assumption that culture can't be measured is simply not true.

3

Data, Data, Data

Most conversations about culture start, and often end, with the conclusion that culture is intangible, impossible to measure and compare, and its progress hard to track. This can be a convenient way of relegating culture to 'low priority' status for leaders in a hurry to achieve 'tangible' results. There are two aspects to the measurement of culture. Firstly, can we profile and measure a set of cultural dimensions that combine to create a unique, definable and prevailing cultural environment? Secondly, can we measure the impact of culture on performance and is there evidence to support this causal relationship?

The answer to question one is a resounding yes, as we shall explain conceptually in this chapter, and in detail in the next chapter. The answer to question two is also yes, and there is a myriad of research evidence to support this conclusion. In my experience, if you believe that culture is the enabler of performance then you won't need much evidence, but if you don't, there probably won't be enough evidence in the world to change your mind. Nevertheless, I will try.

The basic assumption that culture can't be measured is simply untrue

Culture may not be a science in the sense that hypotheses can be proven to 99% certainty with causes and effects linked directly, but culture *can* be measured to a level reliable enough to understand the enabling and disabling characteristics. As always with diagnostic exercises, the quality of insights depends on the basis on which data is captured. In the 1980s, Geert Hofstede and his team captured national culture insights using a five-dimensional culture model. The five dimensions are listed below:

1. Power distance (Low score being egalitarian vs high score being hierarchical)

2. Individualism (Low score being collective vs high score being individualistic)

3. Masculinity (Low score being feminine vs high score being masculine)

4. Uncertainty avoidance (Low score being flexible and relaxed vs high score being controlled and disciplined)

5. Long-term orientation (Low score being short-term vs high score being long-term)

Hofstede used a statistical regression analysis to allocate every country surveyed into a scale from 0–100 for all dimensions, with the mid-point of 50 being the cross-over from low to high scores. Subsequent and additional data has forced a scale beyond 100 for some dimensions in some countries. Importantly, each dimension was theoretically discrete from the others and could be viewed in combination or isolation without any one dimension directly impacting on another. In theory, any high/low combinations of the five dimensions could exist.[2] In practice, certain combinations are rare, as we will discuss later in the chapter.

My Redpill business partners and I read Hofstede's book, *Cultures and Organisations*, in 2012 while preparing to launch our own culture consulting company. We were blown away by the insights Hofstede had gleaned from his national data and the way the dimensions combined to create a complex, but logical, web of cultural characteristics. We were fascinated how the combination of high Masculinity and low Power Distance could help create a dynamic, market-oriented culture and how the combination of high Power Distance and high Uncertainty Avoidance resulted in controlled bureaucratic hierarchies (which may not be everyone's cup of tea, but were often the perfect culture for effective execution, for example, the military). We started to think how this might apply to, and be adapted for, the workplace, and gradually over the next five years developed our seven-dimensional model of organisational culture.

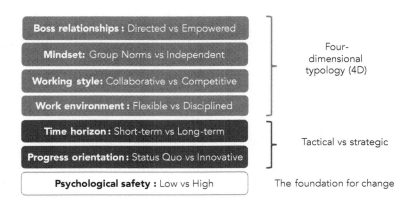

---

2   G Hofstede, *Cultures and Organisations: Software of the mind, Third Edition* (McGraw-Hill Education, 2010)

There are subtle differences between the Hofstede model and the Redpill model, but a student of Hofstede will easily understand the adaptation for organisational purposes. The first six Redpill dimensions operate *without judgement*, meaning neither low scores nor high scores are deemed inherently better than the other. Dimension seven, Psychological safety, operates in a way whereby the higher the score, the better. The models can be compared as follows:

Hofstede model	Redpill model
Power distance	1. Boss relationships (Empowering vs Directive)
Individualism	2. Mindset (Group-oriented vs Independent)
Masculinity	3. Working style (Collaborative vs Competitive)
Uncertainty avoidance	4. Work environment (Flexible vs Disciplined)
Long-term orientation	5. Time horizon (Tactical vs Strategic)
	6. Progress orientation (Status Quo vs Ambitious)
	7. Psychological safety (Low vs High)

The Redpill diagnostic model is made up of thirty-five questions (five for each dimension) and takes respondents about twenty-five minutes to complete. Each question is asked from two perspectives:

1. How do you view the 'current reality' within the organisation?

2. What do you believe your 'strategy requires' to be successfully executed in the future?

I have dedicated the whole of Chapter 4 to explaining this model in detail for those of you interested in the underpinning logic and belief system.

What we believe vs how we behave

We call our culture diagnostic StrategyQ. This is deliberate, to emphasise that organisational culture should always be seen as the *enabler of strategy*. Respondents are asked to answer the questions using *sliders* in an intuitive way and not overthink the implications of any answer. We are trying to simulate how people think in real life, for example in a meeting, when we react to stimuli quite spontaneously. Because of this, participants are often a little shocked at how they answer certain questions, especially when they look at the corresponding dimensional descriptors and how they, as individuals, compare to their group or team. We recently observed the MD of a large organisation select an answer of ten for a question where the zero descriptor was, 'We should care for and support our employees when they make mistakes,' and the ten descriptor was, 'We should aim to win and if we fail, we should try again.' His colleagues unanimously thought the 'required culture' answer should be in two to four range. He responded by agreeing and implied that there must be an 'error in the system'. He didn't like the way he'd answered the question, but his behaviour for the next two hours consistently reinforced that supporting people when they make mistakes was not his way of working; nor part of his belief system. We eventually tackled this conflicting *declared belief* and *displayed behaviour* within the group, and throughout the subsequent culture workshops this particular leader gained deeper self-awareness about the culture he creates, and how this is at odds with the beliefs of his team (and maybe even the needs of his entire organisation). Needless to say, few mistakes were being communicated to him and his understanding of organisational issues was superficial at best. His lack of empathy for mistakes resulted in him not hearing about them at all. This is an example of where the beliefs and displayed behaviours of the leader are in conflict with the beliefs of the rest of the team. In this situation, most teams adapt to the needs or beliefs of their leader, at least in the way they channel their own energy towards their leader. In other words, subordinates protect themselves by agreeing superficially with the beliefs of their bosses, creating a false alignment. These same people may behave differently down the line with their own teams. When beliefs are in conflict within a team, especially when the outlier is the boss, it is unlikely you will observe psychological safety or consistent culture. When we betray our true beliefs, we rarely behave authentically and find ourselves constantly compromised to the point where our team observe us playing political games.

I've got the data. Where do I start?

Psychological safety is the foundational sense-check of whether an organisation can even embark on a culture change dialogue. Low StrategyQ scores for psychological safety are an indication that you may have unacceptable behaviours being displayed that need correcting first. Psychological safety is the oil in the engine that allows everything else to adapt and change. Without psychological safety, people are afraid. With fear, you will be faced with *self-protection* as the overriding employee motive (see Chapter 7: Safe Is Not Soft).

For each of the seven organisational cultural dimensions, we look at the gap between 'current reality' and 'strategic requirement' and also the consistency of answers, using a simple model of standard deviation. The first task when we've gathered the data is to look for indications of priorities and we find these in two ways:

1. Where big change and high alignment exists. These changes are, in theory, non-controversial and potentially extremely high-impact.

2. Where we see *polarisation* in results, with clusters of low/no change opinions, and also clusters of high-change opinions. These are areas creating misalignment in the team and need a thorough exploration of the conflicting beliefs.

At a basic top-line level, the dimensions can be combined to form typologies, and these can help with internal communication deep within an organisation. For example, the following dimensional combination often exists in 'current' culture profiles (meaning the prevailing culture in the organisation). I have indicated the score range that captures > 90% of examples in our database for each dimension (see Chapter 4: Culture Enables Strategy). Remember, each dimension is scored on a scale of 0–100:

1. Directed boss relationships (score 55–70)

2. Group-oriented mindset (score 30–45)

3. Competitive working style (score 50–65)

4. Tactical time horizon (score 20–40)

5. Low psychological safety (30–50)

The combination of dimensions above is labelled (by Redpill Consulting) as a 'tribal' culture type. Please note not all dimensions are relevant for all cultures. Let's look at this particular profile in more detail. Directed boss relationships imply a form of hierarchy and a group-oriented mindset tells us the type of hierarchy (in this case, a collective group conforming to group norms and protecting harmony with a paternalistic leader making most decisions). The fact that this culture is also quite competitive, tactical (short-term) and has low psychological safety implies it will be extremely results-oriented and probably quite a high-pressure environment. It is also too unsafe to challenge the boss and push back on the pressure being exerted. We are seeing this culture type increasingly in our work. During times of crisis such as the Covid-19 pandemic, leaders often become more 'directive' and 'take responsibility'. After an initial period of care for employees, the emphasis quickly switches to results. As with every culture, there are pros and cons with a tribal type. The pros may be decisiveness at the top of the hierarchy, the quick and effective execution of plans and the apparent absence of conflict. The cons may be that these plans emerge top-down only, and the organisation may fail to learn from mistakes (low psychological safety). Tribal cultures are therefore dependent on the leader always *being right*. They are also, by definition, group-normalised, which can make them less open to diversity and change, and people will rarely be comfortable challenging each other at the risk of disrupting harmony. In summary, tribal cultures tend to form homogenous groups thinking in a homogenous way, waiting for leaders to direct, judge and be accountable.

The most commonly seen future or 'required' culture type is what we call a Dynamic System. Dynamic system cultures have these dimensional requirements:

1. Empowered boss relationships (score 25–35)

2. Independent mindsets (score 60–70)

3. Balanced working style (score 45–55)

4. Disciplined work environments (score 50–60)

5. Strategic time horizon (score 55–65)

6. High psychological safety (score 70+)

Let's analyse this in more detail. Empowered boss relationships mean responsibly devolved decision-making, with the boss acting as coach and guide rather than 'director'. When we combine this with independent mindsets, we can envisage a way of working that provides freedom to people and allocated accountability. High psychological safety gives leaders permission to push hard, but also requires leaders to support their people within a climate where challenge and feedback are normal. A strategic time horizon allows the organisation to focus on its longer-term strategy and not knee-jerk when facing difficulties in the short term. Finally, a disciplined work environment means processes, guidelines and rules will help control the organisation and allow people to operate independently within a frame. Dynamic System cultures require organisations to build capability (in order to empower) and ensure processes are defined in a way that enables individuals and teams to operate freely, but without risking an out-of-control environment (ie, a clear framework).

The shift from 'tribal' to 'dynamic system' is complex, as it requires significant change in almost every cultural dimension. Where do you start? Usually, the standard deviations will be lowest (ie, highest alignment) for psychological safety and boss relationships, and as these are also the most important building blocks for progressive positive culture, this is the place to start. The idea is that the diagnostic data informs and provides a frame for the discussion. You may wish to appoint a 'data checker' for this discussion so that the facts provided by the data are not lost in the opinions of the loudest voices. After a period of three to six months you can start to focus on the other dimensions, building on safe and egalitarian foundations. A follow-up pulse-check of the culture diagnostic can help indicate where progress is and isn't being made.

Ultimately, the data gives us insights and permission to describe cultures in a straightforward and logical way. It also helps with the development of a common language that leaders and managers can use to consistently explain what the journey will look like and what the consequences will be for employees, and themselves (see Chapter 8: Consequences). These typologies are not prescriptive, and the most common outcome is a combination of two 'types' with ensuing descriptors that are unique to the organisation concerned. This is the point in the process when we move beyond the models and definitions and towards a unique culture specific to the future needs of *our* organisation.

More than anything else, the data gives us a framework within which to conduct a dialogue. Leaders and managers of teams can discuss the consequences of the proposed change in the context of their own reality and begin the process of working out *how* to support the core elements of change (the tight agenda) and where there will be a need for country, functional or team flexibility (the loose agenda). This co-creation of team priorities is where the magic happens. Without this opportunity for flex, managers and teams feel dictated to. With it, they feel involved and custodians of their own destiny (see Chapter 10: Tight/Loose).

The data can also provide a reality check. Leaders often answer the 'our strategy requires' questions according to their own *preference* rather than what their strategy actually requires, and this can be a useful piece of feedback regarding how they may already be contributing to, and building, a culture that isn't what their business needs. I recently had a situation where a management board were split regarding future requirements. One cluster defined a strong 'Individualistic' culture typology (see Chapter 4 for a description of individualistic culture), whereby results orientation has primacy and people are expected to take responsibility and accept accountability. Empowerment with consequences, if you like. This group had a score on the 'Collaborative vs Competitive' dimension of 82 – the highest skew to competitive we've ever seen for a group of four or more leaders. They also had a 'Collective vs Independent' score of 76, also highly skewed towards independence. In individualistic cultures, people will collaborate with a motive, and that motive is usually for them to personally achieve results and make money. Everyone is out for themselves in individualistic cultures. These cultures can become highly competitive, 'How much do you earn?' environments whereby people superficially collaborate, but the real underlying belief is that one's top priority is to look after oneself, be competitive and win. High-pressure, highly political and lucrative if you can survive it. Many financial and professional services companies have this type of culture. High-pressure, high-reward environments that encourage the survival of the fittest to make a lot of money. Not for everyone, but without doubt, the true motivation of some.

Understanding our own cultural preferences can help us determine whether we can thrive in a given environment and help us make personal decisions about our future. The mental health impact of working in a culture misaligned with your own beliefs and preferences can be exhausting (see Chapter 17: The Feminine Touch) and usually results in high levels of frustration. Many people I know have been labelled 'under-performers' in one culture only to become 'high-performers' in another. We do our best work when we're culturally enabled and, unsurprisingly, so does a business.

Data is a critical ingredient to truly understanding culture, but it asks the questions rather than answers them. Dialogue informed by data is the critical approach towards self-awareness and team alignment. The data has taken us so far, and now it is time for dialogue.

In the next chapter, you can read about all of the dimensions and typologies in more detail. Maybe you recognise your culture in our model, or maybe the one you aspire to in the future? If you use the link at the end of this book, you can try the StrategyQ survey for yourself and gain instant feedback regarding the organisational culture you experience, and the culture you believe is required within your organisation.

DIALOGUE

Purpose: To understand the importance of alignment as a precondition before embarking on culture change, using data as the reference point.

Usually, senior teams are aligned regarding the type of boss relationships that need to exist in the future. If this is the case for your team, then ask question one below. If alignment does not exist (high standard deviation), then ask question two.

1.   Why are we so aligned regarding the required change in 'boss relationships', but have not pursued this change before?

2.   How do we want our 'boss relationships' to be characterised?

This is the most critical alignment topic and the most important cultural dimension, as it provides the basis for our organisational interactions.

Self-reflection

- Did my personal culture data surprise me? Are there some cultural areas where I espouse different behaviours than I display?

- Are my personal values having a positive or negative influence on creating the culture our business needs?

- In which areas do I need to receive ongoing feedback?

- Do I explore differences of opinion in an open way that ensures everyone is heard?

Adopting a shared language for culture change is fundamental to helping people align.

4

Culture Enables Strategy: The Model

In this chapter, we will look at the diagnostic model developed by Redpill Consulting inspired by Geert Hofstede's original research at IBM.[3] I will explain the model in simple terms by describing the high and low poles of each of the cultural dimensions and the characteristics of consequential cultural typologies so that the chapters that follow have a richer meaning.

The seven dimensions

For each dimension, I will show the generic descriptors for low scores (<50) and high scores (>50). However, where an organisation is in the range 45–55, we would describe the dimension as 'balanced' and may display a combination of high and low descriptors. If a score is <20 or >80, it is likely that the dimension feels quite extreme within the organisation. Extreme cultures are usually dysfunctional in some respects. Of course, this is just indicative and for many reasons an organisation may not be aiming for a balanced culture in any specific dimensional area.

---

3   G Hofstede, *Cultures and Organisations: Software of the Mind*, Third Edition (McGraw-Hill Education, 2010)

BOSS RELATIONSHIPS

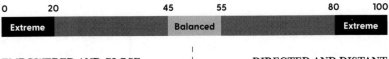

0	20	45	55	80	100
Extreme		**Balanced**		**Extreme**	

EMPOWERED AND CLOSE	DIRECTED AND DISTANT
People act without their boss's direction	Bosses issue instructions and make decisions
Feeling of being equal to bosses	Bosses receive little challenge or feedback
Bosses are available for support	Structures provide people with security
Structures help organise people	Bosses are sometimes inaccessible
Change occurs by evolution	Power holders have privileges
Feedback and challenge are normal	Change occurs by burning platform
Bosses usually go with the majority	Bosses impose their will
People seek and take responsibility	People avoid responsibility

MINDSET

0	20	45	55	80	100
Extreme		**Balanced**		**Extreme**	

GROUP NORMS	INDEPENDENT
'We' mindset – we do things 'our way'	'I' consciousness – 'my contribution'
Criticism spoils harmony	'My' opinions are voiced
Relationships more important than task	Constructive criticism expressed
Obligation to group norms/ways	Honest critique and sharing of views
Shared accountability	Obligation to self
Outsiders may feel excluded	Task prevails over relationships
Heavily dependent on the leader	Individual accountability

WORKING STYLE

0	20		45	55		80	100
Extreme			**Balanced**			**Extreme**	

COLLABORATIVE/CONSULTATIVE	COMPETITIVE
Striving for consensus	Performance and results emphasis
Broad consultations	Win/lose mindset
Involvement of all stakeholders	Focus on speed of decision-making and action
Looks for win/win	Live to work
Decisions more considered	Big and fast are beautiful
Modesty is expected	Admiration for the achiever
Caring and empathic	Need to excel
Being happy at work is important	Being happy at work is a bonus

WORK ENVIRONMENT

0	20		45	55		80	100
Extreme			**Balanced**			**Extreme**	

FLEXIBLE AND LOOSE	DISCIPLINE AND CERTAINTY
Environment is loose and spontaneous	Environment is planned and structured
People trust each other easily	Lower trust until proof of competence
Open-minded	Clarity and detail is needed
Conflict is normal and productive	Priorities and strategy are consistent
Less need for rules	Need for rules and 'ways of working'
Processes are avoided when possible	Processes help to control

TIME HORIZON

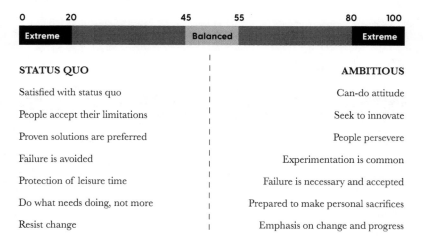

0	20	45	55	80	100
Extreme		Balanced		Extreme	

TACTICAL	STRATEGIC
Short-term business focus	Longer-term business focus
Opportunistic approach	Future has little to do with the past
Quick results required	Rewards are longer term
Rewards are short-term	Strategy more important than quick wins
We do what we've always done	Emphasis on learning and development

PROGRESS ORIENTATION

0	20	45	55	80	100
Extreme		Balanced		Extreme	

STATUS QUO	AMBITIOUS
Satisfied with status quo	Can-do attitude
People accept their limitations	Seek to innovate
Proven solutions are preferred	People persevere
Failure is avoided	Experimentation is common
Protection of leisure time	Failure is necessary and accepted
Do what needs doing, not more	Prepared to make personal sacrifices
Resist change	Emphasis on change and progress

PSYCHOLOGICAL SAFETY

0	20	50	80	100

LOW	HIGH
People may not feel included	We're all on the team
It is not safe to say 'I don't know'	It's safe to ask questions and be curious
People fear being judged	Expertise is appreciated and sought
Problems result in blame	We can all challenge leaders and each other
Expertise not always valued by leaders	We focus on solving the problem
People may behave defensively	Coaching is central to learning

Culture typologies

As discussed in the previous chapter, these dimensions combine to form types. Six of the most common types are outlined below, with the dominant dimensional influences highlighted. In reality, most organisations are not one pure culture, but a combination of a primary and secondary type, so the descriptors may not capture your own organisation in a perfect way.

For each culture type, I have indicated some typical approaches to business and the countries where this type is likely to be prevalent.

Contest culture type – 'Passion for winning'

- Empowered boss relationships
- Independent mindset
- Competitive working style
- Flexible work environment

- Tactical time horizon

- Ambitious progress orientation

Dominant characteristics: Empowered and competitive

General features: Contest cultures have a focus on results and performance and people are comfortable taking calculated risks. They will focus externally on the competition and try to empower their people, especially those closest to the customer. Contest cultures enable quick decision-making with the objective of achieving quick results and improved customer service.

My boss and I: Contest cultures form empowered organisations where people work independently and make decisions proactively. By doing so, they not only grow their competencies, but also influence the business in a real way. Bosses themselves ensure they have enough time for employees, when needed, to ensure tasks are delivered successfully. People will seek accountability and recognition for achievements and will readily give and receive critique.

Employee engagement: Employee engagement is focused on the extent to which employees 'go the extra mile' or 'strive' for their organisation. Employees will be expected to be strong advocates for their company's products and services. Building engagement is focused on personal development, promotion prospects and empowered relationships with bosses.

Influencing the scope of my role: By empowering others, bosses create a climate where people can co-create the scope of their roles. There is usually an opportunity to work on challenging and developmental projects.

Atmosphere: Contest cultures enable the formation of trusting, dynamic and purposeful work relationships. High independence is usually present in contest cultures and manifests itself as a desire to be heard and to express one's opinion. As winning is so important, 'internal competition' may be present, but usually people will be willing to work together to achieve mutual goals.

Innovation: Contest cultures create an open-minded, flexible and experimental environment. Innovation is seen as a priority to win in the market. There is acceptance that some failure and mistakes are an essential way to learn and make real progress.

Bonus system: Contest cultures drive a focus on performance by offering bonus schemes to employees, which in the majority of cases will be based on the combination of individual goals, team goals and behavioural targets. Performance is reviewed openly and honestly and suggestions for improvement may come from anyone in the business.

work–life balance: This element will not be the priority for contest cultures. The key focus is on delivering results, often at a price of working hard and long hours when necessary, but there will be also a pragmatic approach that allows employees to relax when extraordinary effort isn't necessary. The phrase 'work hard/ play hard' may be commonly heard.

Structure: Contest culture organisations have a relatively flat structure, enabling fast and broad involvement of various people in decision-making.

Collaboration: People in contest cultures collaborate when it is required to deliver an outcome or result. Collaboration usually requires some form of 'payback' and people may sometimes be reluctant if this is not forthcoming. It is often necessary for contest cultures to ensure frameworks are built around required collaboration to ensure it happens.

Many organisations that originate from the countries below have contest cultures and it is common for leaders from these countries to advocate contest beliefs:

- United Kingdom

- USA

- Ireland

- Australia

- New Zealand

- Canada

- South Africa

Connected culture type – 'Don't worry, be happy'

- Empowered boss relationships

- Independent mindset

- Collaborative/consultative working style

- Flexible work environment

- Tactical time horizon

- Moderately ambitious progress orientation

Dominant characteristics: Empowered and collaborative

General features: Connected cultures are friendly environments where people value relationships with colleagues and the priority is to feel happy and involved. Consultation will be common, and ideally, decisions will be based on the principle of consensus.

My boss and I: Bosses in connected cultures are close to their employees and enjoy informal and trusting relationships. Employees will offer feedback and challenge to their bosses openly and honestly without fear of reprisal.

Employee engagement: Employees will be primarily engaged by a working environment that is supportive, collaborative and enjoyable. Employees will expect to be consulted about decisions that affect them and to have a feeling that their opinion matters. Having a boss with strong emotional intelligence will be a strong engagement factor.

Influencing the scope of my role: Individual roles will be loosely defined, leaving scope for employees to decide the best way to achieve their objectives. Many objectives will be shared and subject to the way teams decide to cooperate together.

Atmosphere: The atmosphere in connected organisations will be friendly and relaxed. People will support each other when necessary and will generally trust each other and have fun together. Communication will be informal throughout the organisation and will be mostly verbal rather than written.

Innovation: Employees may have the space and freedom to be creative but may lack the processes and discipline to make innovation a reality. Consequently, ideas will be welcomed, but may not always translate into actions.

Bonus system: Rewards in connected cultures are based on a balance of quantitative and qualitative objectives. Targets are often shared by teams and rewards also shared. Recognition may be as much focused on building employee satisfaction as on achieving results.

Work-life balance: Employees in connected companies will enjoy excellent work-life balance and this will be important for everyone top-down. Even poor performance is unlikely to affect the priority of being happy at work.

Structure: The structure will be loose and fluid. Employees will offer their opinions to colleagues and bosses alike and will not be too deferential to seniority.

Collaboration: People in connected cultures will naturally collaborate and see value in helping and supporting others. Collaborative behaviour will feature highly in values and be a critical part of performance appraisal.

Many organisations that originate from the countries below have connected cultures and it is common for leaders from these countries to advocate connected beliefs:

- Sweden
- Denmark
- The Netherlands
- Finland
- Norway

Dynamic System culture type – 'Well-oiled machine'

- Empowered boss relationships
- Independent mindset

- Competitive working style

- Disciplined work environment

- Strategic time horizon

- Ambitious progress orientation

Dominant characteristics: Empowered and disciplined

General features: In system cultures, 'quality' is the most important consideration and results from rigorous processes and clear ways of working. System cultures are performance focused in a controlled way.

My boss and I: Leaders in system organisations are usually approachable and knowledgeable. Employees will respect the leader as a technically qualified person and as a custodian of quality. Feedback will be open and honest and received largely unemotionally as part of the process.

Employee engagement: Employees will be engaged by clarity about roles, responsibilities and how they contribute to the success of the organisation, as well as a feeling that they can provide feedback for improvements. Leaders who listen and provide clarity will be respected and build employee engagement.

Influencing the scope of my role: Roles and responsibilities will be clearly defined. People will be empowered to a degree, but will not exceed their authority limits. Individuals will be encouraged to offer ideas for process and quality improvement.

Atmosphere: The atmosphere will usually be disciplined and dynamic. People will be task-focused and results will be important. People will be engaged rationally, and to some extent emotionally, dependent on the core purpose of the organisation.

Innovation: In system cultures, innovation is often a strong competence. Employees will communicate openly across the organisation and seek continuous improvement. Clear processes will facilitate the development of creative ideas and help bring innovation to market.

Bonus system: In system cultures, people will be rewarded for doing things the right way: working in teams, improving skills and competence, and delivering high-quality results.

Work-life balance: In system cultures, work-life balance is maintained by design. Roles are clear and people are treated fairly, so extreme work demands will be rare.

Structure: Individuals will see themselves as simply one member of a team that needs to cooperate in a disciplined and controlled way. Structures will be quite flat and dynamic, with the rigour and control more defined within roles than by reporting lines.

Collaboration: People in system cultures will collaborate within a defined process, but also exceed these parameters according to individual areas of expertise. People will not compete with each other unnecessarily and see themselves as part of a bigger picture and team.

Many organisations that originate from the countries below have system cultures and it is common for leaders from these countries to advocate system beliefs:

- Germany
- Switzerland

- Austria

- Argentina

- Japan

Hierarchical culture type – 'The boss knows best'

- Directed boss relationships

- Independent mindset

- Competitive working style

- Disciplined work environment

- Tactical time horizon

- Moderately ambitious progress orientation

Dominant characteristics: Directed and disciplined

General features: A hierarchical organisational culture will usually have strong leaders who are highly directive and decisive in style. The organisation will have many tight controls and rules to ensure everyone is clear about their roles and responsibilities so that employees feel safe.

My boss and I: Relationships with bosses will feel quite distanced and a little impersonal. Communication may be formal and instructional. It is rare for employees to challenge or give constructive feedback to their boss in public.

Employee engagement: The primary need for employees will be role clarity and clear instruction from their bosses so engagement is quite rational. Emotional elements may be less necessary, as employees and companies view the relationship as transactional. Fair reward will be important to employees, and if not perceived as fair, may be the biggest driver of disengagement.

Influencing the scope of my role: Roles and responsibilities are usually clearly defined and provide the employee with clarity and boundaries regarding decision-making. The opportunity to influence the scope of one's role will be limited.

Atmosphere: The atmosphere will be purposeful and task-oriented. A degree of intensity may exist and people may be anxious to ensure they are fulfilling their boss's expectations.

Innovation: Hierarchies are task- and execution-focused and may not create the space or time for creative and exploratory thinking, so innovation may often be 'borrowed' best practice.

Bonus system: Individuals will have personal goals and targets and will be rewarded for achieving them. These targets will be quantitative rather than qualitative and will usually aggregate up to the boss's financial objectives.

Work-life balance: Employees will have a transactional relationship with their employers. At work they will work hard and be rewarded appropriately but they may not be prepared to work over and above their contractual commitments without additional incentives. Away from work, employees will switch off and focus on their family and leisure.

Structure: Hierarchical structures are multilayered to ensure responsibility for the execution of tasks is clear and reporting lines are transparent. Matrix organisations will be rare and progression up the hierarchy will depend on the opinion of the boss and delivery of their requirements.

Collaboration: People in hierarchical cultures will collaborate according to the boss's desires. This will often be according to job descriptions and will rarely exceed these definitions.

Many organisations that originate from the countries below have hierarchical cultures and it is common for leaders from these countries to advocate hierarchical beliefs:

- Poland
- France
- Russia
- Japan
- Italy
- Czech Republic

Tribal culture type – 'Join the club'

- Directed boss relationships
- Group mindset
- Competitive working style
- Flexible or disciplined work environment
- Tactical time horizon
- Status quo progress orientation

Dominant characteristics: Group-affiliated and directed

General features: Tribal cultures aim to create and retain harmony and loyalty. Employees are first and foremost part of a group and are supported and rewarded in return for their loyalty.

My boss and I: Bosses in tribal organisations are powerful and respected. They behave similarly to protective and authoritarian parents and enjoy a strong following from employees, who believe their best interests are being looked after. There will be little challenge from employees towards bosses.

Employee engagement: Employees need to feel safe and secure. Employees will feel motivated by being part of a team (family) and will enjoy the safety that is created by co-dependent relationships. Employees will be engaged by consistency. When this is not present, sub-tribes may emerge which may unsettle people and result in tribe-to-tribe criticism.

Influencing the scope of my role: Employees are part of a group and share group norms and group-dependence. The scope of an employee's role will be determined by the boss and individuals will rarely seek to influence this.

Atmosphere: The atmosphere within the 'tribe' will be warm and inclusive. People will feel supported and safe in the knowledge that the main responsibility is taken by the boss.

Innovation: New ways of working will emerge from the boss, so innovation may not be an organisational strength unless it is also a competence of the leader. Tribal leaders may reach out to external experts, as long as the resulting positive impact is attributed back to them.

Work-life balance: The group will do what is necessary to get the job done according to the boss's wishes. There may be times when employees feel under pressure to work longer hours.

Structure: Structures will essentially be the boss and 'the rest', with some people in span-breaking roles for convenience and ease of communication. All decisions of importance will be made by the boss.

Collaboration: People in tribal cultures will collaborate willingly and see themselves as part of a group, but if tribes form at a functional or departmental level, then collaboration across functions may be difficult to achieve.

Many organisations that originate from the countries below have tribal cultures and it is common for leaders from these countries to advocate tribal beliefs:

- China
- Brazil
- Egypt
- Portugal
- Colombia
- Mexico
- India

Individualistic culture type – 'Who wants to be a millionaire?'

- Directed boss relationships

- Highly independent mindset

- Highly competitive working style

- Flexible or disciplined work environment

- Tactical time horizon

- Ambitious progress orientation

Dominant characteristics: Highly independent and highly competitive

General features: Individualistic cultures are usually designed to enable effective employees to become financially wealthier. These organisations may be successful, but can be tough environments where a 'live to work' mentality may prevail.

My boss and I: Bosses will usually be driven and ambitious individuals who may appear to be far more interested in their own careers than their employees' personal development. They can sometimes be excellent people to learn technical skills from, but also be extremely demanding of your time and energy. Bosses will protect their own self-esteem at all costs and cognitive dissonance may be evident.

Employee engagement: The main drivers of employee engagement will be money and status. Employees will willingly work hard, sometimes to the point of burnout, if the size of the prize is big enough. Employees who do not share these values will quickly become disillusioned and probably leave. Individualistic worlds can be extremely divisive.

Influencing scope of my role: Employees will be expected to be self-managed and self-determined. The scope of one's role will be largely down to the individual and will not be questioned as long as results are achieved.

Atmosphere: The atmosphere will be intense and results-oriented. There will be pressure to deliver on time. This may cause some employees to burn out while others will thrive and progress quickly.

Innovation: In individualistic cultures, innovation may be slow because change is threatening to a leader's security and position. Some changes may meet with strong opposition if they do not benefit the leader's local business or function. Innovative or creative people may find the rigidity of the organisation frustrating.

Bonus system: Bonus systems will be generous and almost entirely focused on delivering financial results. Internal competition may result in internal debates about fairness of reward.

Work-life balance: Employees will be expected to do what it takes to get the job done successfully, especially junior employees whose commitment will be tested according to their willingness to make sacrifices.

Structure: There will be a sense of internal competition between functions and departments. Teams will stick together where they have mutual interests, but cooperation between teams may be difficult unless both stand to gain from working together.

Collaboration: People in individualistic cultures may struggle to collaborate unless there is a personal benefit in doing so. Collaboration will be conditional upon a quid pro quo and may be half-hearted in nature.

Practical application

The StrategyQ diagnostic is an intuitive tool designed to evaluate the extent to which your culture is enabling your strategy. For each dimension there are five questions, each looked at from a current and required perspective. It asks respondents to think about the culture that exists today, and the culture required for strategy execution now and in the future. The system gathers a variety of data cuts that can be customised to the organisation in focus. The combination of scores from the five questions allows us to build a dimensional profile looking at absolute scores and gaps.

Once all the data is collated, the overall picture may look something like the following diagram. Current scores are in the light grey oval shapes and required scores are in the black oval shapes.

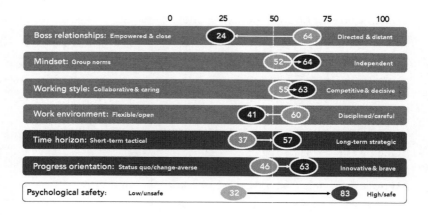

The diagram shows that a big change is required in the type of boss relationships that exist, with a gap of 40 between 'current' and 'required'. Boss Relationships is always the most important dimension, because it sets the tone for so many team and organisational interactions. It is also the most difficult to address, because in many ways it is the most personal and sensitive. Leaders rarely see themselves as 'directive and distant', so this self-awareness is the critical first step for change to occur.

We have now taken the first steps towards culture change: we have asked the questions of our team, they have provided their responses and we have prioritised the change agenda within a simple culture framework. Now we face the difficult step of accepting the consequences, one of which may be that what we personally desire is different to what our organisation actually needs.

Self-reflection

- Do I observe culture with enough insight to understand how different cultural forces interact with each other to create outcomes?

- Do I recognise how my own cultural beliefs are reflected in the decisions I make and the policies I support? Am I open-minded enough?

- Do I have different cultures in different parts of my organisation? Is this causing confusion and dysfunction?

We all bring our own biases to the topic of culture. Therefore, we all need improved self-awareness about how our own beliefs contribute to shaping the world around us.

5

Take Off Your Glasses

In 2012, Fernando Lanzer wrote *Take Off Your Glasses*.[4] In the first chapter of his insightful book, Lanzer explains that to understand the 'world outside', we first need to be aware of our own cultural bias. His challenge was to remove that lens and try to understand different perspectives. I loved the idea that we should all seek to understand each other and be prepared to suspend our assumptions and long-held beliefs.

We've just discussed how we all carry our own paradigms and assumptions of right and wrong and how hard it can be to shift from these long-held beliefs. When we travel to another culture for business reasons or for a holiday, we may experience different cultures, different ways of doing things or different rituals. For a business trip or a short holiday, these different cultural norms can be quite interesting and we may return home to share our newfound insight into other cultures with energy and fascination. These are situations where we are enthusiastically experiencing the *symptoms* of a different culture, in other words, the outward symbols of difference that define others.

4   F Lanzer, *Take Off Your Glasses* (LCO Partners BV, 2012)

Differences can be fun temporarily, but when we actually live and work in another country with different cultural norms, we become exposed to the *causes* of culture (ie, the beliefs that drive the behaviours, rituals or norms). This is when we realise there is a reason for phrases such as 'German quality standards', 'Polish bureaucracy', 'Swedish relationship-building' or 'Anglo-American individualism'. In the 1980s, Geert Hofstede conducted global cultural research by asking the same questions to people working in the same organisation (IBM) about their cultural beliefs. The picture of national cultures he developed is the single most influential study into national cultural differences today and informs much of what we observe in theories and models of modern organisational culture. His findings can be cross-validated by the World Values Survey[5] and many other research studies into cultural differences. One of the cultural dimensions Hofstede explored was called Power Distance, which he defined as follows: 'Power distance is defined as the extent to which the less powerful members of institutions and organisations within a country expect and accept that power is distributed unequally.'[6]

Hofstede found that countries with low Power Distance scores preferred egalitarian worlds, with freedom and empowerment as cultural norms. Countries with high scores preferred hierarchies with top-down direction and decision-making made by our seniors (parents, grandparents, bosses, teachers, priests, etc). On this one dimension, the UK scores 31 (low) and Poland scores 68 (high) on a scale from 0–100. Hardly surprising then that my inclination to empower my team in 2008 was met with incredulity from a Polish

5   C Haerpfer, R Inglehart, A Moreno et al (eds), *World Values Survey: Round seven – country-pooled datafile* (JD Systems Institute and WVSA Secretariat, 2020), https://doi.org/10.14281/18241.1

6   G Hofstede, *Cultures and Organisations: Software of the mind, Third Edition* (McGraw-Hill Education, 2010)

team expecting direction and decisions rather than positively intended questions such as 'What do you think?' and 'Can you provide me with a recommendation?'. I was trying to be *my* definition of a progressive leader, yet they witnessed *their* definition of a weak one. The belief in Poland is that senior leaders should make decisions and be accountable for them, whereas the belief in the UK is that senior leaders should responsibly empower others to make decisions and share the accountability for the outcome. In egalitarian worlds, if the outcome is positive then the boss is supposed to praise his team; if the outcome is negative, then the boss looks in the mirror to see what he or she could have done better. In hierarchies, if the outcome is positive the boss takes more than his (leaders in hierarchical cultures are disproportionally men) fair share of credit for providing the direction; if negative, the team will be at fault and almost certainly have 'implemented his instructions badly'. In both cases the culture works for both leaders and subordinates, because in an egalitarian culture the team seek responsibility and in a hierarchy the team happily defer to the more senior person. Everyone (in theory) is happy, because the behaviour is understood, expected and predictable. The problems tend to arise when the egalitarian, empowering boss enters a hierarchical business, or a hierarchical boss enters an egalitarian business, or (heaven forbid), a merger takes place. Then you may have a clash of cultures which needs insight, self-awareness and active empathy. We have only considered one of several cultural dimensions. If you look at the consequences of the other six (in our model) relevant culture dimensions also being in conflict, then you can imagine how disastrous and complex this clash may become. A cultural personal preference diagnostic should undoubtedly be part of every senior level appointment process, but it rarely is and we constantly hear of examples of failed leadership in cross-cultural organisations.

When two cultures collide, the usual outcome is entrenchment. Both parties genuinely believe their perspective is correct, when in reality neither is right nor wrong. They simply possess strongly held opposing beliefs and so both dig their heels in. If we could just get our heads around the last few words of the earlier sentence... *neither is right nor wrong*... bingo. The motive of the other person is not to frustrate, nor disagree for the sake of it, nor be uncooperative. They simply see the situation differently based on decades of reinforcement at home, school, work, church and with friends. When people from two cultures clash, but need to find a way of working together, the only way forward is self-awareness, dialogue, empathy and shared goals.

I am fortunate and privileged to meet many organisational leaders in my work. Often, the conversation starts with a request from the CEO or HRD for me to help them engage their leadership team on a journey. Usually, this *journey* consists of some aspirational characteristics such as accountability, proactivity, innovation, focus on results, a 'can do' attitude, or greater competitor focus. The initial conversation usually goes something like this:

CEO: I need help to engage my team on a transformational journey.

Me: Is the journey defined?

CEO: Of course.

Me: Who defined this journey?

CEO: I did.

Me: How did you define this journey?

CEO: It's based on my success at my previous company.

Me: Why do you think it will work here?

CEO: Sorry?

Me: Why do you think it will work here?

CEO: It's obvious what's needed here. That's not what I need your help with.

Me: Are you prepared to at least consult with others about the journey?

At this point, the conversation goes one of two ways. Either the initial breakthrough is made and the work begins, or the conversation ends with polite platitudes and we never meet again. To be honest, it's about 50/50.

The CEO does not intend to harm anyone. They are simply using their experience and deeply-held beliefs as a shortcut to find and impose a well-intended solution. After all, the reason they are in the role of CEO is because they've been successful elsewhere, right? The mistake the CEO is making is to assume the same solution will fix the apparently familiar problem. If the culture diagnostic advocated in Chapter 1 is completed, we often see the leader of a business as an outlier (sometimes the only outlier). Their perspective is often the most distant from the organisational reality. Dependent on the existing culture, they may not hear the bad news or be aware of issues that their teams discuss daily. The leader often perceives the organisational culture through the filter of their team; the message may be softened a little for senior consumption or distorted to distract attention away from the sensitive area. The higher up we go, the more openness we depend on, so the safer our environment needs to be (see Chapter 7: Safe Is Not Soft and Chapter 18: Sh!t Happens). However, we often observe exactly the opposite. Some bosses hear what their team believe they want to hear. At the extreme, we see parallels with the fable of 'The Emperor's New Clothes', with subordinates fawning over their boss and reinforcing their words. More often, we observe just enough positive strokes to reassure the boss that their vision is the right one. By completing a culture diagnostic, we can see areas of alignment and indications of any outlier perception. The self-awareness that insights into our own cultural beliefs can bring is often quite shocking to leaders and also the first step to safety and meaningful change.

We all bring our own biases to the topic of culture. Therefore, we all need improved self-awareness about how our own beliefs contribute to shaping the world around us, especially as we enter a discussion about change.

You can use a reliable, beliefs-based culture diagnostic to profile the beliefs and consequential behaviours displayed within your organisation and those that are required to successfully deliver your strategy in the future (for example, StrategyQ from Redpill Consulting, or the Organizational Culture Inventory from Human Synergistics).[7] You may choose to run this diagnostic deep in your organisation to really probe whether there is alignment horizontally across functions and vertically through the levels. This is a vital step in defining current and future culture and should be capable of providing these benefits:

- A profile of current culture existing in your organisation (individual and group awareness)

---

7   R Cooke and J Clayton Lafferty, 'Organizational Culture Inventory' (Human Synergistics, no date), www.humansynergistics.com/change-solutions/change-solutions-for-organizations/assessments-for-organizations/organization-culture-inventory, accessed 9 September 2022

- A profile of the culture required to execute strategy (individual and group awareness)

- Areas of alignment and misalignment, ie, where are the quickish wins? Where are the entrenched barriers likely to be?

- Areas of minor change, major change or no change

- Establishment of a language to frame the culture discussion

- A read on the psychological safety in your business

In parallel, run a series of structured interviews with a sample of leaders (30–50% of top three levels) to gain insight into the language, examples, stories and legends (myths) that people recount. People often talk about situations that occurred several years ago involving people no longer with the organisation. This casts a cloud over current ways of working and the reputation of teams many years later. Our ability to sense-check these historical symbols of culture and consider their relevance in our current situation enables us to assess how difficult certain changes might be and how valid currently held assumptions may be.

 DIALOGUE

Purpose: For the selected 'culture leaders' to gain an understanding of the data and start to sense-check their interpretation. This is the most critical dialogue of the culture change process.

Having completed the cultural beliefs diagnostic, the leadership group should review the results (both their personal perspectives and those of the group). The facilitator should first check that these results can be shared transparently, or whether they need to be anonymised, and then lead a discussion:

- Present the results to the group simultaneously. (Try not to share in advance or give the 'heads up' to anyone, including the CEO/MD/HRD.)

- Check their understanding of what the results mean. What characterises 'current' culture and what characterises 'required' culture?

- Do the results resonate with the group? What examples can they give to reinforce?

- Any surprises? (These can often show where blind spots exist or where seniority gets in the way of the truth.)

- Have a priorities discussion about aligned areas of change and no change.

The priorities discussion is critical. This needs to cover areas that are both important for strategic execution and achievable within a reasonable timeframe. This will require delicate facilitation as it will inevitably take individuals in a direction they do not personally prefer and/or a direction that they are likely to personally struggle with from a behavioural capability perspective. There are many deflection tactics to be aware of here such as, 'My team will struggle with this,' or 'Do we need to consult this with head office?' Both are indications that the individuals are doubting themselves. Key here is to recognise these differences of opinion and ensure enough support and patience are provided. For some the change will be easy and aligned to their personal beliefs, for others the opposite. What is critical is that the senior team move forward at a similar pace, if possible, but even if not, that they are aligned advocates of the changes agreed.

Self-reflection

- Do my personal culture results resonate with me?

- Are there areas of personal misalignment with my peers?

- Am I holding any unhelpful cultural beliefs that may be restricting the growth of my team or organisation?

**For culture to change,
both behaviours and
ways of working need
to change in parallel.**

Yin And Yang

Sometimes, the elements of change have to be managed sequentially, sometimes it's critical that they are managed simultaneously. Culture change requires a 'yin and yang' approach. We've referred to the behavioural and process/practice aspects of culture change several times. Behaviours are things like *taking responsibility* or *challenging constructively*. Processes or practices are things like our decision-making process or our performance management system. Our cultural beliefs affect *both*. If we believe empowered employees are likely to be more productive, we will embark on a development journey to ensure employees have the skills to be responsibly empowered and granted more decision authority. If our decision-making process doesn't enable those decisions to be made by the person intended, then we have a situation where the *process is blocking the behaviour*. Without changing the practice or process, the behaviour will not change either.

As an example, a Polish retail client had an objective of becoming more client-centric and improving customer service in their stores. To achieve this, they had to change practices such as their returns policy and complaints procedure, as well as the behaviours displayed by customer-facing staff, which needed to be more solution-focused and proactive. The process change enables the behaviour. I'd go so far to say *demands* the behaviour. There's literally nowhere to hide when internal processes require our new behaviour to work. Empowerment without an aligned decision-making process provides a hiding place for employees who don't want to take responsibility, or leaders who don't want to let go. Process change without behaviour change creates a bottleneck that highlights a lack of behaviour change. I call this the yin and yang of culture change.

Let's look at a few examples of how positive behavioural intent can be blocked by a disabling process or practice:

- You will not *empower* people if your *decision-making* process leaves authority at the top. This is the most common yin without yang. Many leaders advocate empowerment and even encourage their people to take decisions and to accept more accountability, but unless the decision-making processes are redefined to embrace this change, it is unlikely that decision-makers will actually change. This requires us to redefine who is now accountable for the 'decision' and, critically, who needs to be consulted before the decision is made and who needs to be informed.

This new matrix will create a frame for decision-making and simultaneously ensure the appropriate people are still involved in the process.

- You will not *coach* people if your *1-2-1 meeting agendas* only focus on tasks and deliverables. We're all super busy people trying to balance multiple conflicting demands on our time. You, making time to coach a colleague may be their top priority, yet 'optional' use of time for you. The self-discipline of placing 'coaching' at the top of the 1-2-1 agenda is fundamental to enabling your team to develop and change their behaviour.

- You will not encourage *risk-taking* if your performance management process is *focused on punishing mistakes.* Until mistakes are seen as an inevitable and necessary outcome of taking risks and are treated in the same way as other forms of learning and development, we will probably not encourage risk-taking. If you want risk-taking, experimentation and learning, then you need to positively acknowledge and appreciate the bravery and opportunities that arise from the honest declaration of mistakes.

- You will not drive *behaviour change* if you only *recognise and reward results*. An integrated performance management approach including both behaviours (inputs) and outcomes (outputs) ensures employees focus on both. In other words, we place culture alongside strategy and results in our priorities. The consequence of this balance is that managers can be equally as focused on poor behaviours as they are on poor results.

- You will not create a more *empathic culture* if your recruitment and succession planning processes *focus only on masculine behaviours.* To drive a balance of feminine (f) and masculine (m) cultural values, we need to recognise the feminine qualities in our assessment of employee overall performance. Include 'tolerance (f)' and 'forgiveness (f)' alongside 'challenge (m)' and 'action (m)' (see Chapter 17: The Feminine Touch).

When we begin a process of culture change, we need to manage a cluster of co-dependent behaviours and ways of working so that we deliver a real change and drive different outcomes. The most common reason for failed culture transformation, other than a lack of commitment and alignment among leaders, is organisations pursuing an agenda of behaviour-driven culture change without changing their ways of working. In reverse, the most commonly quoted reason for the failure of digital transformation projects which usually redefines every process affected by the new technology is, you've guessed it, a lack of parallel behavioural change.[8]

During many culture change discussions, I have been advised that certain topics are 'off the agenda'. This usually means they require decisions higher up than the most senior person present can take, and the particular leader wants to lead this change process without involving their own superiors. This can be motivated by many things, but most commonly the leader knows that up-the-line change will be difficult and controversial for their own line manager. Take decision rights for example, or bonus schemes, or intolerance of 'bad' behaviour. All of these can be sensitive topics, but absolutely *must* be addressed for the culture change

---

8   C Sato and R Wang, *Digital Transformation Study* (Constellation Research, 2018), www.constellationr.com/research/constellation-research-2018-digital-transformation-study, accessed 1 November 2022

to be credible down the line and have any chance of success. By avoiding this discussion as a leader, you are simply providing your team with a reason why the culture change will fail, and they will point to your own lack of bravery as the reason for their own failure. Considering all stakeholders and influences on the group is a critical part of ensuring both behaviours and ways of working can work together.

 **DIALOGUE**

Purpose: For the culture leaders or team to practise using the beliefs/behaviour/ways of working model focused on real business issues.

Select a desired outcome, eg Innovation. Then discuss with your group the beliefs that they need to adopt to drive this outcome. Finally, discuss and prioritise both the behaviours and ways of working that flow from the beliefs and deliver the outcome.

Suggested discussion stimuli:

- What beliefs will underpin our desired outcome of being *innovative*?

    - Probe why each belief is important.

    - Ensure alignment by asking each participant why they believe this is important. Testing the connection between the belief and the outcome will show their degree of alignment.

- What behaviours will be evident if we hold these beliefs?

- Check alignment by ensuring the interpretation of how each behaviour will be displayed, for example, there are multiple interpretations of 'empowerment'.

- Align on consequences in two ways.

  1. When the contrary behaviour is displayed – how do we react?

  2. When the desired behaviour is attempted but fails – how do we react?

- What changes to ways of working are required to enable the new behaviours?

  - Decide how new processes and practices will be redesigned.

  - Agree how other stakeholders (especially our superiors) will be consulted.

  - Agree internal communications to support the change.

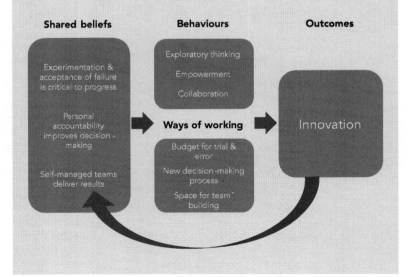

Conduct this exercise a couple of times using different but related outcomes to ensure you have approached the required change from all perspectives. Even one of these holistic thought processes demands a lot of work and a complex change for the organisation. New ways of working need careful crafting and broad consultation, but without these critical enablers, your advocated culture change will be futile. This is where leaders put their money where their mouth is. Behaviours can be advocated and encouraged without huge cost to the business, but new performance management systems, budget allocations and team-building activities all come with significant cost. The facilitator of these discussions should be an experienced person with broad business knowledge – someone who will leave no stone unturned as the new processes and behaviours are being designed and aligned. This person also needs to be an impartial mediator who does not bring their own cultural biases to the table. Once you have the beliefs aligned, you always have a fallback position from which to build the discussion again. Your beliefs become your go-to place when changes of behaviour or ways of working become controversial.

I remember a salesforce transformation process while in the role of regional MD at Coors Brewers in the 1990s. We had embarked on a process of upskilling salespeople to become account managers. Historically, the beer business had been based on relationships between sales representatives and pub or club owners. Customers bought from their 'mates' and beer was generally sold at full wholesale price, plus a tiny discount which every customer was encouraged to believe they were the only ones receiving. This was fine during a period of several decades' growth, but in the 1990s the beer market started to decline, became more competitive and net margins were under pressure. We believed this required a more commercially astute sales organisation able to negotiate more effectively and sell 'brand' value. We wanted to move from selling beer volume to selling the right portfolio of brands at the right price. We wanted to give our account managers P&L responsibility and increased decision authority. A huge undertaking and one that was likely to take years, not months.

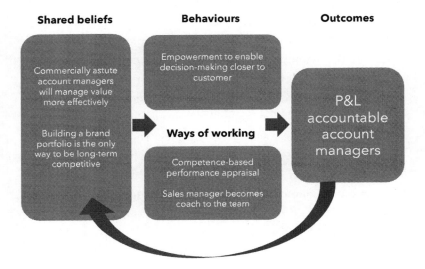

Over the course of the next two years, I was part of a genuine salesforce transformation. Processes, ways of working (including organisational design) and behaviours all became intertwined in a complex change programme. It was probably the most successful commercial change journey I have been part of during my thirty-five years' experience. The change worked for three reasons:

1. Leaders stayed true to their beliefs, which served as the rock on which we depended when times were tough and doubts crept in. Every time we started to doubt ourselves, the CEO would direct us back to our beliefs.

2. Behaviours and ways of working were changed in a parallel and complementary way. Yin and yang were aligned.

3. We were patient with our salespeople, especially those for whom this transformation was most challenging. We created development programmes that were owned and delivered by regional sales managers, whose roles had transformed from supervisor into coach and guide.

Let's take a look at another example. This time, the desired outcome was for leaders to *prioritise culture change*. That may not sound like an outcome, but it was the first critical step of the journey for this particular client. There is little point defining success in transformational terms if the extended leadership team isn't aligned and bought in. Sensibly, this client decided the first six months would be about this outcome. The first barrier was the belief about ownership of culture. Most level two leaders (reporting into management board) believed culture was a soft topic that should be owned by HR and should be provided as a 'service' to the organisation in the form of training assets. The critical element was to gain consistent alignment in the group of thirty leaders that culture was part of all of their roles. In truth we didn't spend enough time stress testing this belief – at best, we had fifteen of the thirty bought in (and as I will describe later, this was not enough). The second critical belief was that 'culture is an enabler of strategic execution'. Again, there was good buy-in from most, but I discovered later that several leaders were adopting the opposite belief, in other words, *get the results right and the culture will become good*. These are the words of leaders who do not believe culture is important and is simply a desirable, but not critical, outcome of success. A year into the transformation, the result was a multispeed organisation. Not one process or practice had been adapted to enable new behaviours (eg, decisions still needed escalation) and half the leadership group were actively driving behaviour change while the other half did not. The half that was trying hard were hitting problems in two ways. Firstly, no enabling ways of working existed (no yang), and secondly, when they were working in cross-team situations (ie, every day), their team found themselves working in a misaligned way to other teams. Culture change failed and the cynicism of some leaders was reinforced.

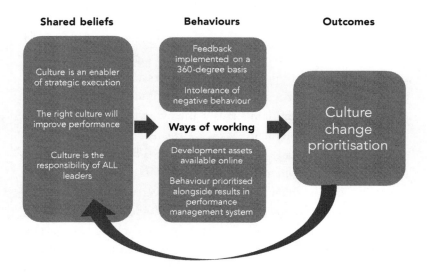

Rock-solid beliefs form foundations

The lesson here is not to move beyond beliefs until you are absolutely sure you have consistent and complete alignment. As an old boss of mine used to say, 'We will work this through until there isn't even the thickness of a piece of paper between us.' *The process of culture change is iterative and ongoing.* We should accept that we will continuously identify 'working practice' changes that are required to embrace behaviour change and vice versa. There may occasionally be an external or immovable barrier to making this change, for example, the involvement of a particularly controlling leader that makes the behaviour change unsafe or practice change impossible. While we can try to influence this situation, we may not be able to change it and we may need to accept some realities. This does not mean the culture change is abandoned. It simply means we remain determined to show its effectiveness in other areas.

There are, arguably, further aspects to culture change that also need to be considered if we intend to manage the change holistically. For example, organisational design is viewed by many as critical to enabling culture. Organisational design serves, first and foremost, to organise your people into dependent and co-dependent groups and can provide some important foundational characteristics for communication and relationship-building. In organisations where management spans of control are too broad, or levels in the hierarchy are too many, we are creating a solid barrier to executing change. I consider organisational design as one of the 'ways of working' you review rather than a separate enabler. Behaviours and working practices dwarf organisational design when culture change is sought. One of the classic mistakes currently being made by organisations is the appointment of 'Directors of culture'. This fundamentally misses the point that culture is owned by all of us, not one person or department.

Self-reflection

- Do I discuss 'beliefs' with my team *before* discussing change so that we are truly aligned?

- Do I manage 'change' holistically, recognising the need for changes to both behaviours and ways of working?

- Do I see 'culture' as an integral part of my role as a leader?

Pressured environments only elicit fear for people if they are also unsafe.

7

Safe Is Not Soft

We've looked at why culture change is fraught with difficulty and why we need to suspend judgement and be open to others' informed beliefs. We've also started to think about the scope of our change journey from a cultural dimension perspective (Chapter 4: Culture Enables Strategy) and a behaviour/ways of working perspective (Chapter 6: Yin And Yang).

All change requires an environment that is safe for people to change within. It requires some existing basic interpersonal freedoms that allow people to experiment with their aspired-to cultural norms. The term commonly used to describe this condition of interpersonal safety is 'psychological safety'.

The great misconception about psychological safety is that it is all about comfort zones and political correctness. While this may be a convenient reason for some to avoid investing time in creating safe environments, it misses the fundamental purpose. Leaders sometimes see psychological safety as optional, a topic that gets addressed when we don't have a thousand other things on our plate. Something to get to when the pressure is off. This usually means these leaders never get to it at all, because the pressure is never off, right? The irony is that safe environments give us permission to be demanding of our people, because when they're safe, they don't feel threatened by our drive for results or our healthy dissatisfaction.

Pressured environments are only likely to elicit fear if they are unsafe for employees.

Safe environments are inclusive, allow us to learn from ours and others' mistakes, enable us to contribute to our fullest and allow us to challenge up, down and across the organisation. The combination of high safety and high drive delivers high performance and learning. High drive without safety simply creates anxiety and fear.

High safety + High drive = Performance + Learning

With reference to our earlier section about the belief/behaviour/ outcome model, a belief that 'safe environments allow us the freedom to be demanding' drives behaviours of transparency, problem-focused learning and healthy challenge. These behaviours drive outcomes of learning and capability development, with problems getting solved quickly and blamelessly. By comparison, a belief that 'psychological safety is a soft HR topic that gets addressed if, and when, the pressure for results is off' may drive behaviours such as a fear of failure or avoidance of risk, with consequential outcomes of blame of others and a lack of transparency of mistakes, leading to repetition of the same errors in the future.

Psychological safety is not something you can announce to an organisation like some divine intervention. Recently, a leader introduced a psychological safety workshop I was facilitating by saying, 'This is a safe environment. You can and should be honest with your views. What gets said in this room stays in this room.' You could hear a pin drop. The silence was screaming the exact opposite. The safety scores for this particular team were very low and the leader had rightly decided he needed to act, but wrongly decided to announce the existence of a safe environment.

The key message here is that change doesn't happen at the moment the insight occurs. This particular leader wanted positive change and was provided with some sobering feedback from his team that informed him the business *he led* was unsafe. The consequence of this was that people felt unable to share sensitive information with him and problems rarely surfaced so that learning could take place. This prompted a laudable determination to do something about it, but the process of change and constructive dialogue *starts* with this insight, it doesn't end there. Our teams will tell *us* when the environment is safe, we cannot tell them (see Chapter 11: Abracadabra).

Psychological safety is a baseline requirement

When you visit the hospital with a health issue, the first thing the doctor does is check your blood pressure and conduct some basic examinations. They do this before starting to diagnose your problem. Same with culture change. Before embarking on any culture change process, you need to ensure the team, function or organisation is healthy and safe enough to cope with it.

This is not to say that low psychological safety is a showstopper for culture change. As a leader of the culture transformation in your organisation, you will need to gauge whether psychological safety is adequate to embark on other elements of culture change, or too low to contemplate it. Either way, understanding the level of psychological safety in a team is a good place to start, especially if you are a recently appointed leader of a team and perhaps not yet seeing the full picture. Questions you may consider are:

- Is this team a safe place?

- Is everyone included?

- Is everybody listened to?

- Is it OK not to have the answers?

- Do people in this team challenge each other and accept challenge positively?

These are just a few of the questions explored in the Redpill psychological safety diagnostic, SafetyQ – a ten-minute survey that may save you months of wasted effort. We developed this tool using the basic construct created by Timothy Clark.[9] The only real difference in our approach is that we see the four areas of safety – inclusion, learning, contributing and challenging – as dynamics happening in parallel rather than his approach of seeing them sequentially. Either way, this is a useful model of approaching psychological safety and can often pinpoint the area of safety creating the barriers for your team.

We are also indebted to the brilliant work of Dr Amy C Edmondson,[10] who explains how safety overcomes fear and releases the potential of people, teams and organisations. Edmondson begins her book with a powerful example of unsafe vs safe environments in hospitals. She conducted some research with the aim of showing that those hospitals that made least mistakes

9   T Clark, *The 4 Stages of Psychological Safety: Defining the path to inclusion and innovation* (Berrett-Koehler Publishers, 2020)

10 A Edmondson, *The Fearless Organization: Creating psychological safety in the workplace for learning, innovation, and growth* (John Wiley & Sons, 2019)

performed best. What she found was exactly the opposite. Those hospitals that performed best made the *most* mistakes. This, of course, is counterintuitive and, needless to say, there was a deeper explanation. The reality was that the high-performing hospitals were *declaring* the most mistakes. Those that performed least well didn't make fewer mistakes, they simply *declared* fewer mistakes due to a lack of psychological safety. Maybe there are moments in all of our careers when we have made this basic error of judgement and accepted the absence of mistakes at face value. How many good teams have we judged a little harshly because their mistakes were transparent, and conversely, over-praised poor teams apparently making fewer mistakes?

Comfort zone	High performance
Apathy	Anxiety

Psychological safety →

Drive →

4 box performance/safety grid. Adapted from *The Fearless Organization: Creating psychological safety in the workplace for learning, innovation, and growth* by Dr A Edmondson (John Wiley & Sons, 2019)

The absence of psychological safety is often a hidden disease within a team or organisation. I use the word disease deliberately, because it causes dis-ease. Depending on the prevailing culture, it may be something that is either dismissed as non-urgent and not critical to performance, or something we simply don't wish to admit to lacking because of our own role in creating it. 'Good news culture' is a phrase we hear often when talking to businesses, especially in the UK or US. In these countries, 'competitiveness' is usually a strong characteristic. Indeed, Hofstede's work in the 1980s found that the UK and the US were both very masculine (competitive in our language) and very individualistic (self-opinionated). Positioning yourself as someone experiencing problems and personal failure is probably not the way to climb the ladder, and climbing the ladder, of course, is important in these countries. *In our experience, leaders in the UK or US are some of the least well informed regarding problems, mistakes and failure.* Scandinavia reflects the opposite. Scandinavian businesses are usually very feminine (supportive and caring) and individualistic (open and opinionated) so we see more safety and supportiveness in response to people being open about mistakes.

We have often conducted interviews with members of leadership teams where they openly express genuine fear of raising mistakes, but when the group is together, this fear is not articulated in front of the boss (especially if the boss has already announced that 'this is a safe place'). This is obviously because the group is not safe. How does the boss get to understand the reality? How does he or she see their own role in creating it and how does the fear cycle get broken? This is where a great boss, honest consultant or skilled facilitator can add enormous value in helping leaders to become more self-aware.

My moment of brutal self-awareness

In 1995, I was the MD of a brewing business based in Yorkshire, UK. I was thirty-two, immature, ambitious and had all the answers. I thought leadership was about confidence and competence. I was half-right. I read Jim Collins' book, *Good to Great: Why some companies make the leap... and others don't*[11] and Tom Peters' book, *In Search of Excellence: Lessons from America's best-run companies*[12] and felt inspired by the concepts of BHAGs (big, hairy, audacious goals), 'hedgehog principles' and 'bias for action'. Leadership seemed to be about inspiring others, always having an answer and making big, impressive presentations with, well, big hairy audacious goals and an attitude of 'just do it'. To an extent, it was. I was successful, sold a lot of beer and earned decent bonuses, but I had this feeling that my legacy would be one of pushing people too hard for performance to be sustainable and perhaps putting my own interests ahead of others. When my boss conducted my annual performance review, I knew it was going to be a good one. I'd smashed the targets when few others had. I was feeling confident. We met at Newcastle airport, and after some polite exchanges, he delivered the words I'll never forget. 'The other MDs have a grudging respect for you, Kev.' The rest of the discussion is a vague memory. I could look forward to another year in my role, but my colleagues (many of whom had decades more experience than me) didn't like me much and experienced no meaningful cooperation. Little did I know, but my (over) confidence was a source of discomfort for others. I was difficult to challenge because I was so certain of everything I said. I wasn't a team player. I was devastated by the words of my boss. In that moment, I started the process of building safe environments, where learning could be a two-way process of mutual respect and my protective armour could gradually dissolve, allowing peers and subordinates to challenge me safely. In a nutshell, I started the long process of

---

11 JC Collins, *Good to Great: Why some companies make the leap... and others don't* (Random House Business, 2001)

12 TJ Peters and RH Waterman, *In Search of Excellence: Lessons from America's best-run companies* (Profile Books, 2015)

leadership maturity which continues to this day. He was the best boss I ever had, and he delivered the most important message I have ever heard. Eight years later, he was promoted to CEO and he appointed me to the management board as sales director. I have rarely felt more appreciative and appreciated. Sometimes, we just have to hear it. Who will tell you?

Psychological safety and diversity

We have explored how psychological safety underpins performance and learning and how it gives permission for challenge and drive for results. It is also a critical enabler of other changes, such as diversity. Earlier this year, Dr Amy Edmondson, together with Henrik Bresman, conducted some research[13] looking at how diversity affects team performance. Most people believe diverse teams perform better than homogenous teams, but previous research had actually discovered the opposite: that diverse teams perform worse than homogenous ones. This could be due to communication challenges, trust issues, different behavioural norms and many other factors. Basically, historical research shows that we usually work better with people similar to ourselves, where we simply feel more comfortable. On average, demographically diverse teams have a negative effect on performance. Edmondson and Bresman wanted to test the effect of psychological safety on this apparent contradiction of diverse teams. They selected sixty-two drug development teams within six pharmaceutical companies with a variety of diversity. They measured diversity using a composite index (including gender, age, tenure and functional expertise) and psychological safety using an established survey measure.

13 H Bresman and AC Edmondson, 'Research: To excel, diverse teams need psychological safety', *HBR* (March 2022), https://hbr.org/2022/03/research-to-excel-diverse-teams-need-psychological-safety, accessed 5 September 2022

Psychological safety is a foundational condition for positive culture change.

What they found was that on average, diverse teams underperformed, supporting the previous insights and conclusions. However, critically, on average, the teams selected were not safe. When they added the impact of psychological safety in the mix, they found that safe *and* diverse teams outperformed safe and 'not-diverse' teams. Therefore, pursuing diversity without psychological safety is probably pointless, but pursuing both in parallel will most likely optimise performance. This makes sense. If you impose change or diversity metrics in an unsafe environment, you will further disrupt a dysfunctional team.

Of the sixty-two teams surveyed, only ten met the criteria for psychological safety. That's just 16%. When we consider the number of organisations that are pursuing diversity (most of them), we can easily conclude that most organisations are probably acting in a way that will harm their performance. Let me restate that. *On average, pursuing diversity in your organisation will harm performance.* This may be an acceptable price to pay to create a more diverse organisation, but I doubt many CEOs would accept this as a probable outcome.

How to create psychologically safe environments

In my experience of helping teams and organisations develop psychological safety, three factors emerge as key. Firstly, the *positioning or framing* of discussions. How we position the challenge, the discussion and the solution. Let's consider two approaches to a discussion related to annual bonus payments in an organisation that's just missed its targets.

Positioning 1: It's been a tough year and we've missed our targets, but I'd like to hear your opinions regarding whether or not we pay a bonus this year.

Positioning 2: I'd like to hear opinions regarding whether or not we pay a bonus this year. It's been a tough year and we've missed our targets, but I have mixed feelings about it. It's not an easy decision and need to listen to each other's opinions fully before taking a decision. I'm sure some of you are equally as conflicted as I am, so let's explore the options openly. Ultimately, we're unlikely to all agree and that's OK, as long as we go away with a decision we can all support.

Positioning 1 sees the leader trying to prompt an open discussion. The leader is seeking to listen to the opinions of the group, but the main point is that targets have been missed and the implication is that this is the most important factor. To some extent, a judgement has been made. Positioning 2 creates a much safer environment for discussion. The leader admits that he or she is conflicted, giving permission to others to feel similarly. The leader implies that there are several areas to explore and that he or she is open to hearing them. Positioning 2 is safer.

The second ingredient for psychologically safe environments is *humility*. Saying things like, 'I'm struggling to think through this problem, I could really do with your help,' or 'You're usually balanced in this type of discussion, whereas I tend to be a bit judgemental. Could we work it through together?' helps build safe environments. Humility is one of those words leaders often associate with softness, but somehow (and ironically), do not find the strength to display. In a 2004 article examining humility as a strategic virtue, Vera and Rodriguez-Lopez define humility as, 'Primarily the ability to make a realistic assessment of one's own work and success; to put oneself into perspective and provide a realistic assessment of merit.'[14] They go on to define some of the traits of humble leaders. You will quickly notice that these are also characteristics of safe teams. A humble leader:

- Is open to new ideas

- Wants to learn from others

- Avoids being self-obsessed

- Respects others

- Wants to help others develop

- Uses mistakes to learn from

- Avoids flattery

- Takes success with modesty

- Has a desire to serve

- Seeks advice from others

- Knows their own limits and wants to correct mistakes

The third factor to help teams and organisations develop psychological safety is the need to be conscious of the *'little things'* we do – those unconscious mannerisms that others see, but which we may remain blissfully unaware of. The raised eyebrow, the smirk, the frown, the eye-roll or the tapping of our pencil. It is important to ask a trusted colleague to hold us accountable for these killer expressions. They shout negativity to our team-mates, and the more hierarchical our environment is, the more these tiny symbols of disapproval matter and harm others.

---

14 D Vera and A Rodriguez-Lopez, 'Strategic virtues: Humility as a source of competitive advantage', Organizational Dynamics, 33/4 (2004), 393–408, https://doi.org/10.1016/j.orgdyn.2004.09.006

Psychological safety is a foundational condition for positive change, whether that change be culture- or diversity-related. Increasing the level of psychological safety in your organisation gives you permission to drive the business harder, not softer.

 **DIALOGUE**

Purpose: To establish if a state of psychological safety exists in your team or organisation.

Facilitate a discussion based on the psychological safety quadrant earlier in the text. Try to gain a consensus on where teams sit on this quadrant by asking the group to consider various working practices, for example, group meetings, 1-2-1 meetings, learning from mistakes, etc.

Self-reflection

- Do I behave defensively when challenged? If so, do I know why?

- Do I actively include everyone in discussions to ensure all inputs are gathered, or do I assume people will say something if they have something to say?

- Do I demand performance from people in a way that helps them feel safe, or do I sometimes leave them feeling worried and fearful?

- Do I display tiny symbols of disapproval towards others?

As leaders your job is to demonstrate a willingness to change yourself, not make big statements and then supervise the change in others.

8

Consequences

Considering the consequences of our actions is something we learn as a child. If we hit someone, they will probably hit us back. If we don't share our sweets, we may get told off by a parent for being selfish and sent to our room to reconsider our behaviour. Culture change is no different. When we decide to do something or change something culturally, there will be inevitable consequences. We will be taking away from some and giving to others, playing to the beliefs and strengths of some and challenging the beliefs and capabilities of others. It is surprising that the people who most commonly fail to consider consequences are the very people advocating the change: our leaders. The changes being pursued are often theoretical positives based on the latest leadership hot topics doing the pseudo-expert circuit on LinkedIn (apologies for my cynicism). This is the populist approach to culture change, whereby we are trying to appeal to our employees by addressing the latest craze without thinking through the consequences for either them, or ourselves.

Let's consider a situation where the leader of a sales organisation thinks they want their employees to take more responsibility, make more decisions and be more accountable. The team may also seek more responsibility, more decision-making authority and want (in theory at least) to take accountability. Hallelujah. The perfect match. Both parties are agreed that this is the way forward.

Not so fast. First let's look at the consequences for the team. They may require more training to understand how to make decisions within a reasonable framework, and they may become more insecure due to carrying the additional burden of accountability. Do they all have the knowledge and skills to succeed? Does the leader need to empower some and not others (creating a more complex decision-making process)? There will be several challenges. None are insoluble, but most are likely to have an associated cost.

Now let's consider the boss. They have let go of decision-making at a certain level, have less control and less visibility of their entire organisation, and are suddenly having to reinvent their role and be more 'strategic'. This may also require training, learning and discomfort. But they're not good at strategy, they're good operationally, and suddenly (in their own mind at least), they lack conviction as a leader. Most importantly, how will they react when mistakes or bad decisions are made and things go wrong that may have been avoided had they been *in control*. There is, of course, an overwhelming temptation to step in, fix the problem and show why they are the boss in the first place. The consequence of this is damaging humiliation for the new decision-maker. The opportunity for coaching and learning has been sacrificed for the irresistible opportunity to show everyone 'how good we are'. There will inevitably be times when the risks involved require this direct intervention, but these will be the minority, and knowing when to step in and when to resist is one of the key aspects of leading culture change.

The consequences of culture change are nearly always harder for leaders to adapt to than for employees deeper in the organisation (assuming we have an acceptable level of safety in place). Usually, the change starts with top-down leadership behaviours being redefined to support the culture journey. Typically required competencies may include 'emotional intelligence', 'responsible empowerment' and 'constructive challenge'. This often brings a performance focus on behaviours, which is good and positive, as long as the organisation backs this up with development assets to support the change. This has two additional consequences. Firstly, you have to invest. Secondly, you have to be patient. Two more bitter pills for leaders to swallow. Your employees will invest a lot more commitment in your culture journey if the capability development is there to support them. I would advocate that if you have provided the necessary support and safety, and show sufficient, but not limitless, patience, you can subsequently be demanding of both behavioural standards and performance outcomes.

When we debrief a leadership team regarding culture change, we always position the change in terms of consequences for employees, for leaders and for stakeholders. Leaders usually understand their role in supporting others through the change, but less so the support they will need to sustain the change in themselves. Most leaders think of culture change as a top-down process that, as usual, requires 'strategic' guidance from themselves followed by 'implementation' from managers and employees. It is one of the ironies of culture change that the strategic bit is actually the easy bit. Most middle and senior managers, given an hour or two of facilitated discussion and some data to reflect on, could define the 'big picture' culture that the organisation needs. Implementation is the tough bit, and it starts with the CEO and their team. A common issue six months into culture change is that, while the top team is advocating the same change as previously, they themselves have not changed at all.

As leaders, your job is to show a willingness to change yourself, not make big statements and then supervise the change in others.

When we stay involved as leaders, when we try, and fail, and try again to change our behaviours, we are both empowered and empowering. Empowered to be intolerant of those that are cynical or uncooperative and empowering others to start a similar process of positive change. If we become the symbol of persistence and learning, we inspire others to follow the same path. If we become the symbol of self-denial and opt out, that's also what we inspire and empower others to follow. When ex-UK Prime Minister Boris Johnson attended a 'party' at No. 10 Downing Street during the Covid-19 lockdown, that's exactly what he gave permission to the fifty-five million people he was leading to do as well. If we behave in a way that positions us 'above' the rules, we essentially define a hierarchy that allows each level to find and exploit its own advantage over the level below. In doing so, we reinforce the culture we started out trying to change. This is one of the most common reasons culture changes fail and, ultimately, our current culture prevails. Maybe we shouldn't be surprised, after all, we created it in the first place.

Some consequences of culture change can be predicted and some less so. For example, some people embrace the new culture quickly – maybe a bit too quickly. They may start to challenge bosses openly, maybe a bit clumsily, so not always coming across as constructive. Perhaps they'll take decisions beyond their empowered level. They are testing the boundaries without having developed the skills to do so effectively. In this situation it is easy for the cynics to say, 'Told you so,' and for a negative narrative to emerge. This is where leaders need to recognise the difference between 'behavioural' and 'ways of working' consequences. The eager employee is trying to behave the way they've been encouraged to, but perhaps without the necessary training or the ways of working being in place to provide the frame. In this situation, applaud the intent, recognise the problem with organisational process and practice, and encourage the brave employee to carry on.

Consequences vary at organisational levels

Your employees are faced with different challenges and consequences at each level in the organisation. Your senior team need to adopt and attempt the new behaviours and support the new practices and processes. Some will find this easier than others and the pace of self-development will vary across the team, with consequences for each leader's team. Middle and senior managers face an additional challenge. They will also be expected to adopt the new behavioural norms, but they will have been less involved in developing them, and so less invested. This group need careful onboarding, and the development assets to support them must be easily accessible and highly effective. This group typically have an additional challenge. They will be expected to coach and help develop their own respective teams, potentially before they have mastered the new behaviours themselves. This is where an understanding of where individual strengths lie is critical, so that managers can be role models for some behaviours and eager learners of others. The willingness for middle managers to work as a peer group and help each other out will accelerate the development process and help develop the important concept of teaming (see Chapter 16: To Team, Or Not To Team).

In my experience, the most likely unforeseen consequence of culture change is people choosing to leave the organisation. Some people simply will not be able to adapt to the new behavioural norms or build the new skills required. Some will judge the outcome before you've even begun and some will be active resisters of the new culture before taking the decision to leave. One of the most important activities to conduct at the outset is an analysis of attitude and energy to ensure you properly understand the reasons for resistance before you judge individuals (see Chapter 15: Do They Get It? Can They Do It? Do They Care?). If you cannot change the attitude of high-energy/poor-attitude individuals who are not recoverable through communication and training, you definitely cannot afford to keep them.

 **DIALOGUE**

Purpose: To ensure consequences have been considered prior to embarking on culture change.

Facilitate a discussion with your team or group using some of these questions:

- Have we considered the consequences of culture change for ourselves?

- Have we created a plan to ensure those 'must keep' employees will stay engaged?

- Do we fully understand our ongoing role as leaders of the change?

- Are we ready with changes to 'ways of working' to ensure behaviours can change?

Self-reflection

Ask yourself the following questions to see if you've personally considered the consequences of culture change:

- Have I considered and embraced the consequences of culture change for myself?

- Do I fully understand my ongoing role as a leader of the change and recognise where I'm a role model and where I'm an eager learner?

- Do I advocate the new ways of working or resist them sometimes?

PART TWO

IMPLEMENTING CULTURE CHANGE

If performance is an ongoing priority for the CEO, then so is culture.

9

Part-time Leader

I hesitated before writing this chapter. Few leaders deliberately pay lip service to culture or their leadership responsibilities or actively sabotage an organisation's culture change, but I have witnessed the premature end to too many culture journeys not to recognise the most common cause. A leader's job is complex: results to achieve, shareholders to keep happy and balancing short- and long-term strategic considerations to name but three. In my opinion, none of these is more important than the leader's role as culture custodian. You may have heard the cautionary phrase, 'Culture eats strategy for breakfast,' but what does this actually mean? My interpretation is that without an enabling culture, a strategy will be hard to execute. Culture should be right up there with strategy on the CEO's agenda. In the words of my good friend, Dan Hammond of Squadify, 'The CEO better make sure they don't become the mid-morning snack by *opting out* of culture change.'

The ultimate leader of the business (usually the CEO) will show the organisation what is important without even opening their mouth. Their visibility, where they show up, their non-verbal communications and their body language will all contribute to defining what is important to any individual leader. When they choose to speak and not speak; when they defer to experts and when they don't; when something is on the meeting agenda and when it's not. Some leaders see culture change as a means to an end. I have some sympathy with this attitude, because culture should never be changed for the sake of it and should always be the key enabler of strategic execution, but it should never be a reluctant voyage or a kind of 'necessary evil'.

Culture change is slow, so it's not usually an attractive option if there is a shortcut to hand. If we offer leaders a three-year culture journey to develop behaviours, capabilities and financial results or a new technology that will deliver the same financial result in twelve months, we all know the likely outcome of the board meeting. However, implementing a technology change isn't just about technology. These transformational projects usually require new ways of working, new skills, maybe some new cross-functional areas of cooperation between users of the same process, and all of this may need – you guessed it – culture change. Culture is constantly quoted as the biggest barrier to the successful implementation of new technology platforms, so the next time you're considering culture as an 'either/or' decision, think about the consequences of the *easier* decision and the culture change it may require.

Culture is constantly evolving

When results are good, not many CEOs look at culture change as a priority. Yet, this is exactly when culture should be re-examined in the context of medium-term strategy. If your strategy evolves to adapt to market needs, so must your culture. If competition intensifies, your decision-making processes, capabilities and behaviours may all have to change too. Not many hierarchies are also innovative and not many bureaucracies are also agile. What drives success evolves over time, even several times in one business in one decade. So, why would we think culture doesn't need to evolve too?

CEOs cannot dip in and out of culture every five years when problems emerge. If culture is only seen as a solution to a problem, leaders will always be playing catchup and reacting to the present challenges. If culture is seen as the ongoing dynamic enabler of strategy, then it will be a permanent item on the meeting agenda, constantly on the CEO's priority list and always part of the lead team's goals

A common issue with culture change is that, all too often, it is seen as a soft HR topic and disconnected from driving performance. This begs the question: when is it a good time to develop culture? When business is good, or when it's bad? If you don't believe that culture is a driver of performance, then neither, it seems. I'm reminded of the time I was proposing a developmental programme to a CEO. Our conversation went something like this:

Me: How's business?

CEO: Unfortunately, not good. We're going to have to delay the leadership programme.

Me: That's a shame. Why?

CEO: We can't be distracted at the moment. We have big issues to address.

Me: It sounds like you need effective leaders.

CEO: We do…

Culture determines your success. It isn't something way down the list that gets done one day when we're 'less busy'. If culture is viewed as a 'nice to have', it will never be in focus. If it's never in focus, you will probably always be firefighting the same old issues. *Ignoring* culture change is actually the soft option.

The part-time culture leaders who see culture change as a 'once every five years' project will probably be the same ones cancelling the leadership programme when business is tough, or cutting the headcount to hit a target in year one, only to incur the costs of replacing these same positions in year three when the business realises it can't cope because nothing else changed when they reduced the headcount. I'm drifting into the sensitive topic of people versus profits, so I'll stop while I'm ahead, but you get my point.

What type of culture leader are you?

Leaders fall into three categories. Firstly, the advocates group who actively support the change, show some personal humility and commit for the long term. The second group are the part-timers. Consequences are rarely considered by this group, because the headlines are the irresistible motivation. The third group are the slow-burners. These are the guys that start sceptical, gradually become engaged and are often the long-term advocates and the great internal examples of change. Groups one and three are hopefully the majority. The problems emerge when the most senior person is a part-timer. I'm being a little harsh here, because part-timers aren't deliberately abdicating responsibility. They are often the catalysts for change in the first place, and they kick-start the process with big announcements, presentations and a lot of internal noise. Then they responsibly hand over to the HR team

A leader who can envision
a culture that is right for the
business, but one within which
he or she may be personally
challenged, is a true visionary.

for them to embed the new culture. The initial part of culture change is the hardest, and often the longest. This involves the senior team learning to role model the change in behaviour, calling each other out in real time when behaviours have lapsed and coping with falling down, getting up again and persevering. They need to be seen to be struggling a little, not always getting it right, and only then do they give permission to the rest of their employees to embark on the imperfect process of culture change. Nothing is more important for a CEO than to be the ultimate custodian of company culture. Note, I don't say 'perfect example of culture change' as this would be a disaster for everyone else to follow. Custodianship requires us to look in the mirror, recognise where we're not meeting the set standards and face up to it. I have deliberately not given leaders permission to opt out of culture or set an example in flagrant opposition to the standards they have set for others (see Chapter 12: Everyone, Or No One).

How to spot a part-time leader

They're usually the strong, confident type. Evangelists on a mission for a few months, who then hand over the 'project' to an HRD, who quickly concludes it's no longer a big priority for the CEO and promptly delegates it to the Learning & Development Director as a 'personal development' project. He or she may be a brilliant L&D leader, but is now somewhat overwhelmed by the enormity of culture. Suddenly, the motivation for the senior leadership team to drive culture reduces. 'The boss has moved on to the next topic, and so should we.' And on it goes. Those who truly buy in keep at it, and those who were sceptical drop out of what has become an optional change process. The problem this creates is that there is no consistency: some leaders are driving culture and some aren't. Employees are confused, and moving from one team to another feels like landing on a different planet. Let me be clear: the CEO didn't intend this outcome (and often re-engages later in the process in an attempt to resurrect the situation), but they haven't connected the need for their personal continuity with the consequences of their delegation.

Strategy and culture are best friends – partners, if you like. They support each other, complement each other and, at times, fight each other for leadership energy. Good. Bring it on. Just don't ignore it.

Leadership does not mean perfection

The CEO does not have to be the embodiment of culture change. We've had many examples of where the CEO is advocate and active supporter, but isn't always best equipped to set the standard. A CEO who can envision a culture that is right for the business, but one within which he or she may be personally challenged, is a true visionary. It's easy to create and evangelise about a vision in our own image. It's much harder to be an honest advocate of a vision that we know will require us to look in the mirror and change fundamentally. I recently worked with an international construction company. The CEO got it. He knew change was important and knew what 'good' looked like. He could articulate it, observe it and wanted to display it. He knew it would be tougher for himself than most, but he stuck with it and persevered. I have huge respect for him. Much more common is the CEO who wants to create something in their own image. They mistake personal preference for business need. In this situation, when their *preferred* culture is communicated and starts to become evident, the assumed benefits usually do not emerge. In this situation, it's more common for the leader to complain about the implementation process than the relevance of their vision in the first place. Culture is then consigned to the 'tried that, didn't work' box and frustration for all continues.

The CEO or leader of culture change has to be prepared for three consequences:

1. The required culture may not match the CEO's own 'preferred' culture.

2. The CEO has to stay involved and committed to the culture journey that emerges, especially if point one is true.

3. The CEO must accept and embrace the personal development and learning consequences of the required change.

What is the difference between 'preferred' and 'required' culture? Preferred is usually just that – a personal preference based on our own upbringing and experience. It is unique to our lens on the world (business and otherwise). It is based on our own beliefs. An organisation's 'required' culture is based on a set of beliefs that enables that specific business to be successful, with success defined as 'successful execution of the business strategy'. This strategy may be short- or long-term, it may require an emphasis on innovation or people or technology, and all of these may require behaviour and practice change within the organisation. It is important, but often difficult, to recognise where the business requirement diverges from our own preference (see Chapter 3: Data, Data, Data).

Once we've identified the required technical capabilities, ways of working and behaviours that will be required in the future, it will become clear that the people responsible for creating the existing culture (ie, the leaders) will *need to change first*. The personal development required of leaders will probably fall mainly into the behavioural space. Within this broad term, there will be conscious (or known) development needs, and secondly, blind spots. The blind spots are critical. Gaining 360-feedback based on the *required* cultural behaviour model can be an excellent way of identifying blind spots, which will usually be scored higher by the individual themself than by others (sometimes much higher).

Once blind spot weaknesses are revealed, the leader has a choice. Either embrace the feedback, start self-development and seek a regular progress report from the business, or ignore them. In our experience, 90% are ignored.[15] That is not a typo. In 90% of cases, the most senior leaders of businesses do precisely nothing about their blind spot development needs. They remain blind spots, no-go areas of personal development. *This means the most important development needs for the most important person involved in the process of culture transformation remain untouched.*

	Self-score low	Self-score high
Others score high	Blind spot strengths	Recognised strengths
Others score low	Recognised weaknesses	Blind spot weaknesses

What can other leaders do about this? In an egalitarian, safe environment, you can do a lot. Firstly, set the example you want to

---

15 Redpill CompetenceQ database

see in your boss. Address your own development needs, focusing on your own blind spot areas. Observe specific examples of the behaviour you believe needs to change in your boss and provide timely feedback about how this made you *feel*. Encourage your boss to implement a process of regular 360-feedback focused on the leadership team's blind spots. More than anything else, continue to reinforce your boss's role as leader and custodian of culture and what that means in practice. Explain how important their leadership example is to the whole organisation and how their reluctance to change gives everyone in the organisation permission to do the same.

In a hierarchical culture that is also unsafe (and this is the majority of large corporates), the challenge is much harder. This is where political networks become important. If you want to influence the behaviour and self-awareness of a senior leader in a hierarchical, unsafe organisation, you need to understand *who* really influences *who*. This is where external support can help enormously. An external consultant is not restricted by hierarchical structures and can influence those closest to the leader by explaining that their personal role is not just to 'manage' their own team, but to create consistency across the leadership team (including the ultimate boss). By encouraging the advocates of culture change to see their role more holistically, we can literally plot how to positively influence the boss.

 **DIALOGUE**

Purpose: To prepare your CEO for the culture change journey and its consequences.

Set up a series of one-to-one discussions between the facilitator/consultant and your CEO. These need to be held at the beginning of the process of implementing change. The CEO should understand that:

- The required change may not be their own preference

- They must be a strong advocate for culture change

- They must be prepared to be a vulnerable learner

- They are to set an example that gives others permission to make mistakes and struggle at times

Self-reflection

- Do I kick-off culture change 'projects' and then move on to more pressing issues?

- Do I hold my boss accountable for the culture changes they may start but subsequently neglect?

- Do I accept and act on feedback that identifies my own development areas?

The challenge we face with any complex change is to ensure we do not compromise our values and maintain a frame within which we can flex if necessary.

10

Tight/Loose

The idea that culture can be carbon copied across functions, countries and regions is at best naïve, and at worst, plain dangerous. The core concept of this book is that culture is the enabler of strategic execution. This has to be constructed and applied in a situationally flexible way. Markets are different, people and peoples are different, regulatory environments differ and working practices can be more or less advanced even within the same company. All of these considerations require us to consider culture in context. There are behaviours we may hold dear to our newly implemented culture, while accepting they may look different in different countries or regions. Step one is to recognise this and allow some loose interpretation of a core behaviour. Step two is where empathy is needed and an understanding that the same word or behavioural descriptor may not mean the same to everyone.

The challenge we face with any complex change is to ensure we do not compromise our values and that we maintain a frame within which we can flex if necessary. I call this the Tight/Loose framework. Within every organisation there will be some 'tight' elements of culture. Usually these will be company values such as integrity and honesty, plus some 'looser' elements such as an organisational intention of being customer-centric. It is easy to see how integrity is tighter than customer-centricity. Integrity requires us to tell the truth, act according to our convictions and be authentic. This will probably not need too much nuancing, dependent on function or provenance. We can almost certainly hold this value reasonably tightly across our entire business without offending anyone or blocking our local execution. We all know what a lack of integrity looks like. When it comes to customer-centricity, we may see variations. In market one we may have a disproportionately online business that requires us to think mainly of the end consumer as our customer. Marketing may be our critical functional competence and decision-making about pricing may be held tight and centrally. On the other hand, in market two we may be in a more traditional route to market with several distribution levels. In this situation, our ability to manage the value chain through several layers of commercial consideration may require looser pricing in the hands of an experienced commercial team attempting to ensure ultimate brand integrity at point of purchase. In market one, the price decision-making is tight and controlled. In market two, price decision-making is loose and empowered. Of course, market two is more complex and has the potential for tension and inconsistency, but this risk is a price worth paying to compete in this market. Complexity usually creates the need for compromise. If we embark on a culture of empowered decision-making, but never really release any central control, we disable our commercial team and frustrate them with our duplicity. If we over-empower them without any control, we run the risk of creating chaos in our brand positioning, resulting in both a dysfunctional distribution network and value erosion.

Watch your language

Language in organisations can also be flexibly interpreted. National cultural norms (and, therefore, organisational norms) influence

Headline words and intentions do not always result in displayed behaviour.

our understanding of behavioural terminology. As an example, let's look at how the word 'empowerment' may be interpreted by a team of competent people:

- In company 1, *empowerment* means you are 'empowered' to implement your manager's instructions, with regular check-in sessions.

- In company 2, *empowerment* means you will be consulted and then 'empowered' to implement what is agreed with your manager.

- In company 3, *empowerment* means you are 'empowered' to create solutions to the problems your manager and yourself agree are the priorities.

- In company 4, *empowerment* means you are empowered to get the job done by finding the problems, deciding what's important and finding the solutions. You consult your manager when *you* think it appropriate.

For someone in company 4, the definition in company 1 doesn't sound like empowerment at all. It sounds like hierarchical, top-down micro-management. For somebody in company 1, the definition in company 4 sounds like a recipe for uncontrolled chaos. Both approaches can work and both approaches may be appropriate for the situation prevailing in that particular business, but we tend to judge each other's cultures as wrong based on our own lens. The skill here is to allow the people working in different functions and markets to tell *you* if they feel appropriately empowered to do their jobs effectively. If the answer is yes, then we shouldn't judge the reality. We can hold a value of 'empowering people' and encourage empowered behaviour without it being identical everywhere. This may look slightly different within one company if it spans several different countries.

Introducing constructive challenge

Another commonly required 'new' behaviour advocated during culture change is what we might call 'constructive challenge'. This may be a simple and positive intention to encourage people to constructively challenge up, down and across the line if, and when, they disagree with another person, irrespective of who they are and what position they hold. The reciprocal expectation is that this challenge is received positively and without defensiveness by the person challenged. Again, the behaviour is highly situational. If you have ever lived or worked in Eastern Europe, you will know that the likelihood of observing a subordinate challenge a senior person is quite rare, and the more senior the person, the less likely it is. In most Eastern European countries senior people, or more specifically, the *position* of senior people should be respected. Subordinates may disagree with leaders, but they are unlikely to challenge them in public. They may choose a moment privately to question a decision without causing any embarrassment to the senior person or 'disrespecting' their position. In a country like the UK, where organisations have strong egalitarian values and close boss relationships combined with high levels of individualism (a willingness to hold and express 'my' opinion), people will often challenge openly. However, the UK is also a masculine country (competitive), so the challenge may often result in an argument and not always be observed as constructive. In Sweden, we see egalitarian values, high individualism and more feminine behaviours, so the challenge is likely to be made, accepted and embraced without defensiveness. This is not to say the UK approach is worse than the Swedish approach, it simply highlights the fact that constructive challenge will look different across companies in different countries.

Implementing a tight/loose framework

There may, in reality, be three categories of Tight/Loose thinking in the initial phases of culture change. It may be necessary to accept that some ideally tight areas are looser in the initial phases than you would like. These may ultimately fall into either the tight or loose category in the future, but initially fall into a temporary, 'in-between' category. The skill here is not to force consistency, but achieve buy-in to the journey and show empathy.

Some examples of typically 'tight' culture change elements:

1. Values of the organisation, for example, integrity and authenticity

2. Psychological safety in all interpersonal situations

3. Core processes, for example, decision-making and performance management system

Some examples of typically 'loose' culture elements. Remember, loose doesn't mean optional – it means locally nuanced to recognise different prevailing norms in country, function (risk or regulatory related) or market:

1. Behavioural requirements, for example, responsible empowerment and constructive challenge

2. Office/remote working arrangements

3. Degree of bureaucracy

By clearly defining tight/loose elements of culture change, we are also by definition defining what we will not tolerate behaviourally. It's important to note this does not define your culture. It simply forms the lower boundary to acceptable behaviour that will have consequences.

 **DIALOGUE**

Purpose: To ensure 'tight' elements of culture are agreed and aligned.

Facilitate a discussion between leaders across the business to ensure the 'tight' elements of culture are clearly defined and aligned and the 'loose' elements are given certain boundaries. Try to agree on a small number of tight elements and a similar number of loose elements for the initial step of the culture journey. Look for quick-win opportunities in data gathered from your original diagnostic.

Tight processes are easier to control than tight behaviours. Tight processes may have decision points, system input requirements and evaluative criteria applied to them. Behaviours are much more complex and require us to hold each other accountable. This means we are obliged to talk about behaviours openly and constructively. The 'how did we behave' conversation rarely appears on the meeting agenda and yet a fifteen-minute conversation between peers about how they have behaved towards each other for the past few hours and how we 'felt' when certain things were said or not said can be valuable shared experience.

 **DIALOGUE**

Purpose: To build self-awareness of individuals in the context of 'tight' culture elements.

Facilitate a discussion in your group focused on the 'tight' behaviours you wish to start (encourage) and stop (no longer tolerate) on your journey of culture change. Ask people to volunteer to be today's recipient or subject and then adopt a simple structure for providing that individual with some honest and specific feedback.

The MYO (My, Your, Our) technique is simple and effective:

M = **My** observations of your behaviour:
My observation was..., my interpretation was..., it made me feel...

Y= What was **Your** intent? (Subject responds with their own intentions explained):
I was trying to..., I was intending to..., I was feeling...

O = **Our** learning

Tight behaviours that will no longer be tolerated should be called out in real time and after a reasonable grace period should have consequences for the individual transgressing. The eradication of anti-behaviour is the most important first step in tight behaviour change. It is a powerful signal to the organisation that things are changing. Ultimately, people who continue to behave badly or disrespectfully, or against the cultural norms defined as tight, should be exited from the organisation, irrespective of how technically strong they are or the results they achieve. This is a powerful statement regarding the importance of culture to all employees who are positively adapting to the new requirements, and makes a bold statement that the behavioural standard is not optional. There are no sacred cows in culture work.

Self-reflection

- Am I clear about the 'tight' aspects of our culture? Or are most elements 'loose' in reality?

- Do I recognise which changes are most difficult and allow an adaptation or transition period before tightening the requirements?

- Am I sensitive to the needs of different teams or functions before determining what is 'tight' and what is 'loose'?

If only culture change was so easy that we could wave a magic wand and declare that the culture is changed, the business is healthy, the employees are happy, and the bonus is bankable.

11

Abracadabra

And then, as if by magic, the culture is changed. 'Fantastic. Well done, everyone. How are the numbers looking this month?' If only culture change was so easy that we could wave a magic wand and declare that the culture is changed, the business is healthy, the employees are happy and the bonus is bankable. Yet, this is precisely what many leaders do. This is not intentional, simply an outcome of the 'project' mentality that frames the culture 'issue' for many leaders. Leaders scope the project, appoint a consultant (sometimes), draw up a timeframe, appoint a project manager and approve a plan. This plan, like any other, then has to deliver against certain milestones.

Culture change usually starts with a genuine intention to address the characteristics of current culture that get in the way of effective business practice. These are well known within the organisation, the subject of 'coffee-machine' frustrations, and deeply established:

- 'We need people to be responsible and take accountability.'

- 'We need more challenge. I want you to challenge me.'

- 'We need less bureaucracy; we need to be agile.'

- 'We need to be more long-term focused, stop constant changes and stay on strategy.'

- 'We need more discipline in our execution.'

- 'We need less internal navel-gazing, more market focus.'

- 'We need simpler ways of working.'

- 'We must learn from our mistakes, not blame each other.'

- 'We need to trust our subject matter experts.'

Sound familiar? This diagnosis, or one quite similar, is common, especially in large multinationals heavy on process and light on agility, who (ironically) may claim to hate process and aspire to agility. The point is that leaders know what they want. They can envision it, describe it and even write about it, but can they lead it? As discussed earlier (Chapter 9: Part-time Leader), leading culture change is not the same as embodying it. You don't have to be the perfect example of what we're talking about, but you do need to be a committed leader-advocate who aspires to the vision and be prepared to learn as you go.

Initiating the change

Once you've agreed that the desired future is sufficiently different to what prevails today, you can start to analyse the changes needed. A typical culture change programme begins with a diagnostic. This needs to be a representative sample across locations, functions and levels, plus a series of one-to-one interviews – a combination of quantitative and qualitative insight that provides a picture of current and required cultures and helps you create hypotheses for further discussion. You then test these hypotheses with a group of senior leaders to establish the shared beliefs that will support culture change and the behaviours and practices that will embed these changes. (We usually create a parallel manager-led communication programme that engages people deep in the organisation and gleans their feedback for consideration and review.) Leaders should begin to embrace the new behavioural priorities and maybe even submit themselves to a 360-feedback process structured around the new behaviour model. There are usually some surprises in the feedback ('peers see us differently to subordinates'; 'the boss seems to rate me higher than I expected'; 'my perceived weaknesses are not as weak as I thought, but my strengths aren't as strong as I thought, either'). In parallel, the organisation should brief the ever-willing learning and development team to build some development assets aligned to the behaviour model. This initial phase of culture change may take nine to twelve months.

If the first phase is characterised by insight, prioritising change and self-awareness, the second is dominated by false harmony. The reality is, by this stage you have probably done a better job of describing to the organisation 'what I don't want to see' than what you do. You definitely don't want to see blame, disrespect and disdain, so these negative behaviours become the focus of attention. People start to consciously control these negative behaviours without fully understanding what to replace them with and a false harmony emerges. None of us wants to be singled out as displaying the 'old culture' behaviours, but the eradication of negative or anti-behaviour does not mean the new culture has miraculously been created. It doesn't even mean the old culture has been corrected. It may simply mean people are now conscious about their previous incompetence. The tension is now personal and internal. 'We have something to say, but we're not sure how to say it anymore.' Now you have to move the organisation on from conscious incompetence to conscious competence. You need to learn safely how to become effective and build a culture that enables the business and doesn't just paint a veneer of positivity over the cracks. You need to move from removing negatives to displaying positives.

These are baby steps towards change, albeit important ones. To many leaders, false harmony can appear powerful and seductive. This is the time to get really clear about the standard you need in the future and see it as the beginning of positive change and not just the end of the bad stuff.

And then disaster strikes

The temptation is irresistible. The leader has a compelling urge to announce what has been achieved so far. The leader calls a 'townhall' and prepares an organisational message that sounds and feels like you've arrived at your destination. The culture change is 'announced' and the magic wand is waved. Unfortunately, the language becomes self-congratulatory and over-assumptive about the degree of change achieved so far. The leader essentially gives themself permission to move on to the next big project, because the culture project is done.

This doesn't apply to other areas of the business, so why culture? You wouldn't announce that strategy is 'achieved', because strategy is an ongoing and evolving topic. It would sound a bit silly, frankly. 'Good morning, everyone. I'm delighted to inform you that we have achieved our strategy.' Now what? The issue with culture change is that it's viewed as a project. Leaders announce the start of it, so they feel the need to announce results. Culture is ongoing. It's the partner and enabler of strategy. It defines the way we work and our behavioural norms. It's the tangible processes and the intangible norms we all recognise. It does not have a beginning and an end. It cannot be wrapped up

Resist the temptation to announce culture change. If true, your people will tell you.

in a box with a bow tied around it and presented to everyone as a gift. Remember the example of the MD who announced that the meeting was a safe place and no one need fear any interpersonal consequences (Chapter 7: Safe Is Not Soft)? The meeting didn't suddenly become safe because the MD announced that it was. It becomes a safe place when the behaviours of the group make it one. Culture change *is not a project*.

Reaping the benefits

When can you reasonably expect to see some of the benefits of culture change? I suggest a two- to three-year timescale for visible and consistent behavioural change, and twelve to eighteen months for key practices to be adapted to enable these behaviours (see Chapter 6: Yin And Yang). Practices and processes are easier, because they're not human. Humans complicate culture change. Realistically, you might be able to directly link your business results to culture change in year three if you're lucky. (By then, of course, you may need a change of culture.)

All of this is not to say some things cannot change quickly. The CEO who changes the management board meeting agenda to include a section on 'feedback' or 'learning', or appoints a nominated 'challenger' whose job it is to play devil's advocate in the safe knowledge that this is their role, will immediately change the way team members prepare for meetings. The idea of nominated challengers, incidentally, can be an extremely effective way of ensuring challenges get raised in a safe way. I used to perform this role for one of the management boards I was a member of and it really made me think about the *consequences* of the proposals being voiced so that I could challenge the prevailing thinking in the moment and with a degree of empathy.

I also used this method when I was managing a large digital transformation project. I nominated the person most likely to disagree with me (she usually did), and while there were times I regretted my decision, without her regular and valid pushback I would have made many more mistakes. Changing the way that you run your meetings is the quickest and easiest way to start your change journey. It shows your intent, places you in a vulnerable position of not being able to fall back on the way things have been forever, and it almost certainly requires people to prepare in a different way. Here's some ideas for you to consider. A couple of these on your next agenda will signal your positive intent:

- Appoint a nominated challenger.

- Rotate the chair.

- Emphasise problem-solving (instead of information updates).

- Speak last as leader.

- Include 'feedback' on the agenda.

- Position discussions with multiperspective outcomes.

- Keep to a maximum of three hours.

- Use a '10% past, 20% present, 70% future' approach to agenda items.

The second way you can make an instant impact as leader is in the way you run your one-to-one sessions with subordinates. Placing the emphasis on them to provide the agenda immediately tells them it is their meeting, not yours. This enables them to determine the agenda. Don't be surprised if the content shifts from 'update and review' to 'development and learning'. Abracadabra. With just two changes to your ways of working, you have started the journey of transforming your team culture, but it will not be easy and requires self-discipline to maintain beyond the short term.

So much of our working day is taken up with meetings these days, changing the way we structure this time and defining the competences required to run them can be powerful.

 DIALOGUE

Purpose: To redesign meetings so that they are enabling your culture journey.

Facilitate a discussion with your group or team that aims to reinvent your weekly or monthly meeting agendas. Ask the team how the time can benefit them most and help them perform their jobs more effectively. Explore alternative ways to update each other so that discussions in meetings can be participative. Ask the questions below:

- How can we become more forward looking?

- How can we all contribute to the agenda?

- How can we become more focused on problem-solving and barrier removal?

- What behaviour change do we want to embed as meeting best practice?

While most aspects of culture change take time, there are certain elements that are strong statements of intent and can immediately shift the emphasis of how we spend our time, especially in meetings. The more these new meeting practices can be consistently embedded, the quicker the whole business will start to adjust its focus.

Self-reflection

- Do I have a clear short-term and longer-term change agenda?

- Do I allow some people to opt out of easy short-term changes, creating inconsistency?

- Am I comfortable changing the way I run *my* meetings?

When leaders find a way of staying aligned, they create trust, consistency, safety and predictability for their employees.

12

Everyone, Or No One

If culture is a set of positive norms that you wish to adopt to help you achieve your goals, together with a clear understanding of what you will not tolerate, then you have to be clear on one, crucial non-negotiable. These norms *must* apply to everyone, irrespective of position. In fact, the more senior the role, the more important the advocation of these norms becomes. I'm writing this chapter in March 2022. In the past two weeks, the UK government has apologised for breaking its own Covid rules and the Australian government has apologised for sexual harassment occurring in parliament. These are two extraordinary own goals. Both governments need the trust of their citizens to exist and operate effectively. In the UK, the reaction of some members of the British public was to angrily opt out of the same rules. In Australia, equality groups quite rightly made hay with the revelations.

In companies large and small, similar issues can often emerge. A board of directors may agree on a culture transformation that requires behavioural change and new ways of working to be implemented. These new behaviours apply to everyone, or no one. Full stop.

Lack of leadership alignment is the Achilles heel of culture change

The most critical ingredient of any culture change is the consistent alignment of the leadership team. They set the tone. They determine whether the stated culture is important or not and they decide whether behaving according to the cultural expectation is, in reality, optional. When culture becomes optional, it often becomes irrelevant or even toxic – one rule for the many, and another rule for the elite. Organisations will gradually see increasingly lower employee engagement and increasingly higher turnover of talented staff. In these companies, 'values' statements become the focus of internal ridicule and external confusion. They become known as the 'poster on the wall' instead of the way we behave daily.

The difference between an aligned leadership team and a team playing according to their individual motives is often the difference between successful or failed culture change. When leaders opt out of cultural consequences for themselves, they kill the change process. In the example above, the disdain shown by the UK government towards its own citizens was seen by many as highly disrespectful and elitist. This is not to say the 'elite' or the 'powerful' actually know that what they are doing is wrong. Sometimes the privilege of position and power makes these anti-behaviours unconscious blind spots that are only addressed when they are caught.

In companies, this is more likely to look like a continuation of behaviour we want to see less of. Take 'micro-management' as an example. If you want more trust and empowerment, you will probably need less micro-management and controlling behaviours, but simply agreeing to more empowerment rarely results in less micro-management. A micro-manager is behaving this way for a reason. It could be their preferred way of working because it plays to a strength of 'attending to detail', perhaps they don't believe the competence of their team is sufficiently developed for them to be responsibly empowered, or there could be a lack of trust between individuals. Leaders then start to build a rationale, stated or unstated, that allows them to opt out of empowering their team and continue the behaviours the organisation is trying to stop.

Helping leadership teams to stay aligned

In theory, the team has agreed the required change and signed up to the medium- to long-term outcome. The challenge now is to reassure the leaders who have some hesitation. In the case of 'empowerment', there is a temptation for leaders to announce this directionally and then communicate 'empowering' messages down the organisation. In other words, they show their commitment to empowerment by using the word more often, but if they don't stop micro-managing, there will be confusion, frustration and inertia.

The most important ingredient to successful empowerment is a process of 'cautious hands-off'. For example, a decision empowered to a team member can have a strong consultation process step with the boss before the decision is made. This will benefit both parties: the boss will stay involved and the subordinate understands what is really important to the boss. As the consultation becomes easier over time, this process can move to telling the boss of an intended decision. Finally, empowerment is experienced when the boss is merely informed of a decision already made. During this process, the subordinate will grow in confidence and competence and the boss will witness the subordinate's approach to decision-making and have the opportunity to observe and assess their capability before letting go. The critical message is that the leader does not opt out of the culture change, but that the team adopts a gradual implementation to meet individual concerns. Without this empathy towards bosses and the acceptance of a gradual approach, there will be a 'some in/some out' approach to culture change.

Most commentators of culture change look at a top-down process of leaders doing the doing and employees being the happy recipients of the new environment. For change to be successful, the consequences are two-way and so the empathy and patience also has to be two-way. If culture change becomes a kind of unofficial way of judging leaders, it can stifle well-intended but failed efforts to change. We should recognise that a new culture is always harder for leaders to adapt to, because they are the ones who created the old one and so they will be watched the closest.

When leaders find a way of staying aligned, they create trust, consistency, safety and predictability for their employees. Whether I work in IT, Finance, Sales or Marketing, I can expect a similar behaviour code and a similar way of working to emerge. If I move departments or functions, I will meet new personalities, but experience one basic culture, albeit with some elements tighter than others.

Culture is not a cloning exercise

Leadership alignment is never easy and staying on message can be a frustrating experience for some, especially those that advocate an independent mindset where people should not be forced into a way of thinking or being. Here, it is important to understand the difference between 'cloning behaviours' and 'adopting cultural norms'. Multiple personality types can, and should, exist within any one culture. For example, extraverts and introverts can both be 'empowering' leaders. Culture is a set of beliefs that are translated into individual behaviours according to diverse personalities, not a set of cloned behaviours we all have to implement according to the same style and script. This accusation of cloning is one of the many objections we hear during culture change processes, usually from people who are highly individualistic. My response is always the same. Carry on being who you are. Share the same beliefs as your peers, share the same desired outcomes, and be the person you are while also being true to the shared beliefs.

In many organisations, a type of tribal culture exists at functional level. Leaders of functions develop a tight team around them and most of their energy goes into developing their influence over this team. These senior functional leaders may encourage their own team members to work with each other, cooperate with each other and build on each other's ideas. However, the same behaviour in themselves would require cross-functional peer group cooperation, and this (in their own eyes) may diminish their power. Supporting a peer when their actions are causing your team problems is much harder than empathising with the complaint being voiced to you. How often does a sales director support the marketing director when the sales guys complain about marketing, or vice versa? This ability and willingness to align with a peer at a senior level is exactly the demonstration of maturity that changes cultures and forms a powerful consistency within the senior team.

Learning from failures

What happens when we mess up? During every culture journey I have been part of, either as a leader or as a consultant, one thing never changes. Every single team I have worked with on culture change messes something up, usually multiple things. The mistakes are never the problem – the subsequent way of dealing with them is. No one expects a leader to be perfect (except, perhaps, the leader themself). We've found two things that work really well to assist early-stage behaviour change:

1. Real-time or near-time feedback from a trusted peer. A raised eyebrow, a questioning look or a subtle, but obvious, smoothing comment can all improve levels of self-awareness in the moment. Some leadership teams actually adopt a signal to alert each other to their behavioural transgressions. Usually, the individual knows exactly what they've done, and now they know others do, too.

2. The apology. Self-awareness that's followed by an apology in the moment is powerful. The apology should not be caveated, for example, 'I'm sorry, I shouldn't have said that, but it just really annoys me when...' This gives everyone permission to behave badly when something annoys them. 'I'm sorry, that wasn't the behaviour I wanted to display, it's not good enough from me,' is far more impactful. Self-awareness, apology and learning is a strong message to everyone that they, too, can make mistakes, but learn and move on determined not to repeat them.

Sharing our own failings is a brilliant alignment tactic. When we share, we give permission for others to share, too. When we fail, we give permission for others to fail, too. Most importantly, when we learn, we give permission for others to learn, too.

Whether culture change succeeds or not will depend on leadership alignment and advocacy. When leaders are misaligned, or worse, opt out, they make culture optional. Prepare for tough times if you're making culture optional. Employees see straight through this 'Do as I say, not as I do' approach and this is where labels such as 'toxic' or 'elitist' start to enter the organisational vocabulary. A simple self-reflection against the advocacy/alignment diagram below can point out the areas you need to work on as a team and as individuals.

	Low advocacy	High advocacy
High alignment	Words without action	Driving culture change
Low alignment	No culture change	Acting on personal agenda

The 'words without actions' leader (or more commonly, 'words with superficial actions') quickly loses credibility. This is the leader who sets up the employee engagement survey, but doesn't act on the results or the leader who creates the diversity forum reactively when the 'ism' becomes a hot public topic. Employees see through this cynicism and only judge these short-term, opportunistic actions in the long term against real change. One leader/organiser of a diversity forum recently told her leadership team after poor attendance, 'There will be consequences for the people that didn't show up for this forum.' An absentee employee told me, 'I've been advocating for gender equality for ten years and suddenly I'm preached to by a "leader" who claims to know everything but seems to know nothing about gender equality. If there are consequences, so be it.'

The 'acting on personal agenda' leader is the most common. There is high advocacy for their own version of what 'good' looks like. This may include some elements of the aligned culture change and some additional elements precious to the individual. Usually, their energy is behind the latter. This type of leader means well, but is a bit narcissistic in their approach. In the short term, some positive changes may be experienced and the internal team may improve their working culture, but as soon as two teams have to cooperate, the differences may become barriers (see Chapter 10: Tight/ Loose). As soon as leaders act independently with 'tight' cultural requirements, they risk creating sub-tribes in their teams, functions or locations. When cooperation with other teams, functions or locations is required, they may face issues, so understanding critical dependencies is vital to culture change success. Sales *and* Marketing; Manufacturing *and* Logistics; innovation *and* market insight: mapping out the relationships at team and functional level to enable your business to operate effectively becomes another important element of 'tight' culture change.

 DIALOGUE

Purpose: To build leaders' self-awareness of aligned and misaligned elements of culture.

A discussion with your leadership team about the way they show their alignment or misalignment can often raise some important issues. Alignment examples are often restricted to desired outcomes (the result we want, the metric that needs to improve). Misaligned areas are often deeper and start to explain why people in different functions receive different messages or why a priority for one team is less so for another. Facilitate the discussion by asking your team these questions:

- Where are we aligned? What does the team observe about this list?

- Where are we misaligned? What does the team observe about this list?

- What mixed messages are we sending?

- What culture are we actually creating?

Self-reflection

- Do I behave as a member of a team or an individual with my own agenda?

- Do I make some 'cultural' and 'behavioural' allowances for some high-performing individuals that I don't make for others?

- Do I agree with decisions and implement them fully or do I agree publicly and then do little to make them happen in reality?

- Do I help others who are struggling with culture change or leave them to become increasingly exposed?

There is sometimes an inner need for leaders to be acknowledged as *the* driver of change rather than being part of an aligned group of leaders.

13

Energy Flow

As a leader of culture change, your role can sometimes feel overwhelming. You are expected to be the perfect role model (which is not realistic, nor necessary) and you struggle with conflicting priorities as you try to adapt to a new reality that places no less pressure on you to deliver results. How you channel your finite energy during culture change is something you need to be conscious of. During change, the vast majority of leaders display what we call vertical energy flow. They channel about 20% of their energy up the line towards their boss and 80% of their energy down the line towards their direct reporting team. This means three groups of people are often neglected: their peers, their peers' teams and themselves.

The vertical leader

The power of peers

During culture change, peer group relationships become important, but they are easy to neglect. Apart from the obvious alignment challenges discussed in the previous chapter, there are a number of reasons that these relationships are important. Your teams will be interacting with other teams. Sometimes, there will be a parallel and complementary change process happening and sometimes not. When you have teams clashing due to culture change (for example, one team is empowered and another is not, but somehow they are expected to work on the same project), then influencing your peers to adopt a consistent cultural approach helps to facilitate working together. This may mean one leader has to slow down a little, or another has to speed up a little. Either way, the leaders have to find a way of helping their teams cooperate. This may even need a little mediation for more senior leaders to find a solution that works. They need to stay focused directionally, with the same ultimate outcome in mind. This may require some compromises regarding the speed of change. If you are the only horse running and you're running fast, it won't be long before there is no one around you to work with.

An example: I was facilitating two psychological safety sessions recently for two functional lead teams within the same organisation. The IT team had made significant progress in the past twelve months regarding employee engagement and functional team safety. The lead team was an excellent example of 'internal' psychological safety: they were learning from each other, challenging each other constructively and performing well. The finance team was not quite as safe, but still safer than most teams, and much safer 'internally' than cross-functionally, even in interactions with IT. This, on the surface, seems strange. Two safe teams in the same organisation, with theoretically the same vision and values struggling to work with each other. The issue was where both leaders of function chose to channel their energy. Both were 'vertical' energy people and focused on their boss relationship and their direct reports as a 'their' team. There is deep irony in this. Both sought safer working environments, both were politically astute and managed up-the-line energy, but both regarded their team of direct reports as the team and both complained about interactions team to team. This is particularly evident in competitive cultures where leaders are competing with each other and tribal cultures where leaders are trying to build and control their own sub-tribes. As leaders, we sometimes mistakenly believe that cooperating with a peer somehow dilutes our role. In fact, in the eyes of most of our colleagues, we grow as leaders when we display the maturity to influence and cooperate cross-functionally.

There is also sometimes an inner need for leaders in competitive cultures to be acknowledged as the driver of change rather than being seen as simply part of an aligned group of leaders. The reality is, in the long term, shared execution is vastly more successful than solo execution. Do you want to share in successful culture change or be the driver of a good effort that didn't quite work?

Supporting your peers

Peers can also be a valuable safe sounding board. Partnering with a peer and providing mutual feedback regarding positive and negative displayed behaviour can be an effective way of keeping calibrated and honest. Leaders should agree at least two peer group feedback partnerships to keep them honest (preferably not peers most similar to themselves).

In larger groups of peers, your role may become one of supporter rather than feedback provider. When a peer is being unfairly judged by a superior or another peer, you could (and maybe should) show your empathy and support in the moment. Again, the likelihood of this happening is culturally influenced. In hierarchies, it would be normal for the group to stay silent when a colleague is being criticised by a boss. The force of 'respecting' the boss is stronger than the force of supporting the peer. In individualistic cultures, unfair criticism may provoke a response of support because the force of needing to express our opinion is strongest. In competitive cultures, this added element of individualism may result in confrontational situations quite quickly, because the purpose of the challenge is sometimes a combination of supporting the peer and *winning* the argument. Of course, you should remain constructive and specific in your support, reinforcing the behaviours you have agreed to be your new norms while trying to distract attention away from the person and towards the problem, thus creating a safer space for the whole team to open up. In more hierarchical cultures, the support may be shown by speaking to the unreasonable boss privately. The critical point is that you show your support and do it in a safe and constructive way. The ability to do this will almost certainly require some coaching, so that you can both challenge and be challenged constructively. In nearly every case of culture change there will be joint perspective of 'giver' and 'receiver' to consider. Give and receive empowerment; give and receive challenge; give and receive feedback, etc. As leaders, receiving will often be tougher, especially when the required outcome is a culture whereby employees start to channel more energy up the line, thereby challenging leaders.

Leadership alignment is the single most important element of successful culture change. I considered making it a separate chapter but decided it will be a running theme throughout the book. Genuine, authentic alignment of peer group leaders, whether they are a board of directors or an extended leadership team, can be a powerful force within the organisation. An ex-boss of mine coined the phrase, 'Member of leadership team first, leader of function second,' to stress to his board how important their alignment and mutual support was. He used to say he didn't want the 'thickness of a piece of paper' between us. We called this 'cabinet responsibility'. Our debates and disagreements were fierce, but our front to the organisation was aligned and we were supportive of each other. In terms of debates, each member would 'win some and lose some'. This resulted in a leadership team that, over time, would have done anything for one another and could not be divided by cynics across the wider organisation. The outcome of strong alignment is obvious: consistent messaging, consistent priorities, mutual support, and most importantly, trust and psychological safety within the group, enabling colleagues deep in the organisation to feel safe.

Prioritise peers' teams

Your peers' teams may seem like a strange relationship to call out as a priority, but never underestimate your influence as a leader cross-team or cross-function. Showing empathy towards the people you and your team have an impact on and cooperate with can be a powerful way of engaging them in pursuing mutual goals. Similarly, inviting peers to engage with your team can help you achieve cross-team alignment and support. When leaders take an interest in other teams, they are sending an important message to them. They are seeking to understand their pressures, which in turn enables them to empathise. This may have a cautionary effect on them the next time they want to criticise the team or department that's 'disabling' their progress. Most leaders don't even direct 2% of their energy towards their peers' teams. This should be more like 10%. That's one day every two working weeks getting to understand your cross-team and cross-functional colleagues. Payback will be swift, I promise you.

Energise yourself

Finally, the most often neglected energy flow is yourself. There are a million books dedicated to self-development and this is not my purpose. This is a straightforward look in the mirror. Take the time to ask yourself questions like:

- What did I do today that I could have done differently or better?

- Which interactions might have had better outcomes?

- Who do I need to apologise to?

- Who do I need to thank?

- What mistakes did I make that I should share with others?

- What do I need to share with others to help them feel safer during change?

Is the force of 'respecting' your boss stronger than the force of supporting your peer?

Our ability to be vulnerable is the most important quality for creating psychologically safe environments. This quality (that would have been classified as a weakness in my early career) has rightly become the most important leadership quality of all, but it requires our own energy and commitment to discover it. Take a good look in the mirror. Do you like what you see?

The way we choose to channel our energy has a significant effect on our own ability to drive culture change. The vertical leader will almost certainly find themselves exposed at times, without enough self-awareness or the proactive support of peers. Culture change, by definition, is a shared goal and no individual can declare independence. The holistic leader understands that.

 **DIALOGUE**

Purpose: To create a consciousness in the team regarding how individuals channel their energy and how peer group relationships can be tightened.

Discuss the concept 'Member of leadership team first, leader of function second' (in other words, 'Peer group ahead of subordinate team'). This takes a bit of processing (see Chapter 16: To Team, Or Not To Team) but it is a useful discussion to calibrate the role of leaders in the organisation.

Self-reflection

- Am I a vertical leader? Where do I need to channel more energy?

- Do I apply the same thinking to 'my' team of subordinates as I apply to myself as a member of a peer group?

- Do I truly understand the pressures of other teams or functions and take account of this day to day?

Our ability to recognise when not to pretend to be the expert in the room and when to listen more and speak less is a sign of our leadership maturity.

14

Pseudo-experts

From time to time, I run a leadership programme for a Swedish client. The programme is focused on a small number of leadership competencies and an appreciation of cross-cultural differences. One element of the programme is a simulated situation whereby a group is to assume the role of plane-crash survivors stranded in the desert with a limited number (fifteen) of items available. The task is to make some fundamental decisions by prioritising the fifteen items to maximise the chances of survival in the desert. At the end of the exercise, a reputable desert survival expert provides the solution according to his opinion. I have never yet run this simulation with either a real-life plane-crash survivor or an experienced desert survivalist present within the training group.

During the task, the people that usually dominate group discussions continue to dominate this particular discussion. They speak with confidence and authority on a broad range of topics and appear to know what they're talking about, but it is often the most vociferous that are the most insecure. They try to demonstrate competence when they are actually filled with self-doubt.

In business situations, some people have an inner urge to try and lead even when they are not qualified to do so. In the case of the desert survival exercise, the object of the exercise is simply to survive. It doesn't matter who leads or who provides the ideas and motivation. The point of the exercise is to use the skills, experience and knowledge of the whole group to agree a solution. Unfortunately, in situations like this, where no one is experienced, the so-called 'pseudo-expert' is at his (it's usually a man) most dangerous.

In his book *Why Do So Many Incompetent Men Become Leaders? (and how to fix it)*[16] Dr Tomas Chamorro-Premuzic explains how confidence is often misinterpreted as competence because of the way we stereotype leadership traits. He writes, 'Confidence – a trait more associated with men – is often misinterpreted as competence. As a result, charismatic, but incompetent men have fewer barriers to reach the top than women.' Chamorro-Premuzic goes on to explain, 'Most of the character traits that are truly advantageous for effective leadership are predominantly found in those who fail to impress others about their talent for management.' Many of the traits mentioned by Chamorro-Premuzic underpin safe and effective change and are critical during culture transformations. The role of women, and more importantly feminine culture traits, as drivers of culture change will be explored in Chapter 17 (The Feminine Touch).

High levels of apparent confidence can be so overwhelming for some people that they feel unable to contribute to the discussion. The confident pseudo-expert is a force to be reckoned with. Challenging someone like this can feel akin to entering unnecessary conflict. Needless to say, most people back off, especially if the

---

16 T Chamorro-Premuzic, *Why Do So Many Incompetent Men Become Leaders? (and how to fix it)* (Harvard Business Review Press, 2019)

'expert' is also the boss. In one desert survival simulation, the misinformed pseudo-expert took the group to almost certain death in the desert. When the real expert played back the solution for survival, there were several nodding heads in the room, implying several silent contributors who may have made a difference to the outcome. The response from the pseudo-expert was to question the reliability of the survival expert, implying he may make exactly the same mistake again.

Creating self-awareness

When you are a confident generalist, you need to be self-aware in three ways:

- Firstly, at what point do you start guessing? At this point, have the self-control to stop.

- Secondly, be sure you don't back yourself into a corner from which there is no escape. Leadership is not about providing all the answers. It's about making sure someone in the room is able to provide an answer.

- Thirdly, the confident generalist needs to realise when he is overriding a real expert.

If pseudo-experts need more self-awareness, then so do genuine experts. Our tendency as an expert to undervalue our knowledge and expertise is equally as problematic as our tendency to overstate our abilities when we have limited skill. Genuine experts need to be heard and need to be encouraged to speak up. This can be a daunting experience for some when asked to contribute within unsafe environments. If step one is a need for leaders to be self-aware about their level of expertise, then step two is to ensure an environment of 'safe contribution' exists that enables true experts to voice their opinion without interpersonal risk (see Chapter 7: Safe Is Not Soft).

Specialists and generalists must co-exist

In organisations that include highly technical departments, the tendency of a confident generalist to second-guess expert opinion is a common frustration. We often see situations where no genuine experts are present in the room when key decisions are made. The leader's role here is to make sure the expert is present and consulted, even if they are not the person making the final decision. This may mean a more 'junior' specialist needs to be invited to more senior meetings. Why is this so difficult for some leaders to accept? The benefits are clear, and there are no downsides, just a healthy blurring of hierarchy. The most obvious example of this working well in recent times is the way national governments and their leaders almost universally deferred to medical expertise during the Covid-19 pandemic, and yet clearly held decision rights and accountability for restrictions. Rarely did the leader of government override the advice of medical counsel. This is also the way it should be in organisations. Leaders should not behave as pseudo-experts. They should take advice from experts and make decisions on an informed basis.

Culture is a topic that everyone feels obligated to have an opinion on, so the potential for pseudo-culture experts to emerge is quite high. A recent workshop of senior leaders with a UK-based retailer demonstrates this point quite well. The MD of the business unit and the CEO of the group were joined by members of the MD's management board. This placed the MD in a tough situation. Boss *and* subordinates together in the same (albeit virtual) room. For the MD, the need to exert influence and the temptation for

Are you allowing confident pseudo-experts to make too many decisions?

pseudo-expertise behaviour was high. During a discussion about leadership behaviours that emerged from the results of a culture diagnostic, the MD made what could have been a conclusive statement. 'We need more accountability and passion for winning. Let's keep it simple and communicate this widely.' Luckily, other members of the group saw the challenge facing the business in a bit more depth and wanted to explore the consequences of the proposed culture change on their teams and themselves. One team member even asked what a 'passion for winning' looked like, saying, 'It sounds like American rah-rah' (apologies to American readers). Superficial observers of culture will always look for the headline or the quick-fix mantra that can be placed at the top of a one-pager and broadcast widely. These leaders are so focused on the outcome that they neglect the hard work required and *their* role in it. It is not a leader's role to simply provide soundbites and move on. When the most dominant voice is also the most confident, most senior and most superficial, there is a problem.

The Dunning–Kruger effect

Part of this issue is that human beings are not good at evaluating themselves accurately. Research has shown that we frequently overestimate our own abilities and those with the least ability are most likely to overestimate their competence.[17] Known as the 'Dunning–Kruger effect', this is:

> 'A cognitive bias whereby people with limited knowledge or competence in a given intellectual or social domain greatly overestimate their own knowledge or competence in that

---

17 J Kruger and D Dunning, 'Unskilled and unaware of it: How difficulties in recognizing one's own incompetence lead to inflated self-assessments', *Journal of Personality and Social Psychology*, 77/6 (1999), 1121–1134, https://doi.org/10.1037//0022-3514.77.6.1121

domain, relative to objective criteria or to the performance of their peers or people in general.'[18]

This knowledge gap can have ongoing impact. Firstly (and obviously), mistakes are made, then learning is missed and then mistakes are repeated. If a leader is trapped in this cycle, they will not recognise when and where they are making mistakes, to the extent that they may deny even having made them. This isn't about ego; leaders simply don't see the errors. This phenomenon may be exacerbated by the corresponding effect of true experts not realising how expert they actually are. The solution to the Dunning–Kruger effect is increased self-awareness. This can be gleaned from 360-competence surveys or direct feedback from others. In other words, if you are arguing with a fool, first ensure the other person isn't doing the same.

Luckily, on the occasion referred to above, the CEO called out the MD and the discussion wasn't derailed. That could have happened had the CEO not been in the room, as was the case a few months later when the same MD *announced* the successful culture change in the business to a bewildered audience. Cultural leadership requires patience, humility, depth, experimentation, support, authenticity, self-awareness and resilience, not headlines and overconfident pseudo-experts.

Great leaders speak last

Your ability to recognise when not to pretend to be the expert in room and when to listen more and speak less is a sign of leadership

---

18 Dunning–Kruger effect definition: Britannica, www.britannica.com/topic/bias-attitude, accessed 7 September 2022

maturity. The same boss of mine that said, 'Be a member of the leadership team first, leader of function second,' always (and I mean always) spoke last. No need to exert himself, no need to control others, just a strong need to listen to everyone's opinion before deciding. Sometimes he drew on one or more of our views and sometimes not. Either way, he listened and considered options before summarising and deciding. He knew when he was the expert in the room, and when not; he knew whose opinions he needed, and for which decision. He was authentic and purposeful almost every time he opened his mouth.

When we enter a process of culture change, we are nearly always facing new challenges or required to behave in a new way, so why do we expect to be an immediate expert? The answer may lie in leadership stereotypes that we create: a leader *should* lead the way, *should* role model the change and *should* become instantly competent. Effective leaders of culture change know when they can role model and when they can be willing advocates, but not yet examples of excellence. This allows the leader to be human and vulnerable. If culture change is experienced as a leader's brainwave rather than an organisational requirement, it will lack substance, relevance and involvement. Leaders are a critical part of the process, but setting themselves up as the personification of excellence and expertise will inevitably lead to disappointment.

Pseudo-experts are particularly dangerous in hierarchies, where challenge is highly unlikely. I am reminded of an example of a client considering a brand repackaging project. The commercial director was the most senior person in the room and an 'expert' on most things. Early in the presentation, he sat back in his chair and stated, 'My wife wouldn't buy this.' The brand manager targeting her brand to twenty-somethings probably thought to herself,

'Great, your forty-something wife is not our target consumer,' but instead of saying this, she sheepishly agreed to go back to the drawing board. Concept killed and pseudo-expert reinforced.

DIALOGUE

Purpose: To help leaders gain self-awareness of where they may be displaying pseudo-expert behaviours.

Ask the team to consider all other members of the team from two perspectives:

- What is this individual's strength you would like to see more of?

- What is this individual's blind spot weakness you would like to see less of?

Self-reflection

- When am I a bit fake? What additional knowledge and competence do I need to build to become more expert in areas necessary for my job?

- What skills exist in my team(s) that I do not use enough? Why do I avoid this?

- Do I know who might be the pseudo-experts in my team?

When your culture isn't changing, don't jump to conclusions about the reasons why.

15

Do They Get It? Can They Do It? Do They Care?

Picture the scene. You're six months into a culture transformation process and nothing has changed. Same problems, same undesirable behaviours, same lack of employee engagement and no real evidence that the new behaviours you so carefully crafted and communicated are being embraced with much, if any, enthusiasm. Leaders seem fragmented and misaligned, managers are frustrated and employees are rolling their eyes at the third failed culture change in five years. As always, there is pressure on short-term results, tasks to be completed, projects to manage and head office information demands to be met. Faced with this situation, many leaders conclude that their employees' attitude is wrong, and culture change is too difficult and takes too long. In parallel, employees conclude leaders will never change and the organisation drifts into a passive mindset of 'told you so...'

There are three main reasons people within organisations fail to change:

1. **Do they get it?** Have leaders and communicators *explained the change* in a way that people understand?

2. **Can they do it?** Do your employees believe they can *adapt to the change*?

3. **Do they care?** Is there something in this change for *them*?

Do they get it?

This is where you explain the basic reason for the changes proposed. At this stage, are you linking the required behaviour change to a strategic imperative? Are you responding to competitive pressures? Are you addressing an employee request? When you explain the change, maybe it sounds like a transitory idea that will soon disappear as a priority (like last time)? Importantly, the first test of change at this stage is communicating with your audience effectively and providing a compelling rationale for change. This stage requires more than your employees simply receiving information. Do they understand the consequence for themselves? Do they understand the change in behaviour you are expecting to see? Critically, do they understand the consequence of not attempting, and ultimately succeeding, in this change?

In Lesley Allman's book, *Better Internal Communications: How to add value, be strategic and fast track your career*,[19] she talks about *informing*, *connecting* and *engaging* your audience before expecting behaviour change. Her model is a great way to explain step one of the process (do they get it?) and, to some extent, step three (do they care?), because it includes the 'understanding' and 'motivational' elements of communication in the 'connect' stage. Allman states:

---

19 L Allman, *Better Internal Communications: How to add value, be strategic and fast track your career* (Rethink Press, 2021)

'To simply provide information, use one way "tell" channels... such as apps, intranet, emails, posters, newsletters, podcasts or videos. To connect with your audience will require a bit more time and involvement... such as conferences, meetings, town halls, webinars and huddles. Finally, to engage with your audience, you will need to involve them. This will inevitably take more time. For this, you need two-way channels that are more about listening than telling... such as workshops, focus groups and skip-level meetings.'

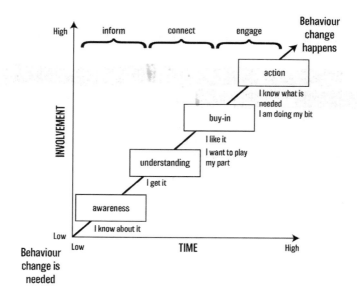

Can they 'do' it?

Once you can tick the, 'Do they get it?' box, you move to step two. The second reason people may fail to change is due to a held belief that they lack the capability. They ask themselves, 'Can I do it?' Changing behaviour or building new skills is not automatic. It isn't something people can switch on and off. Behavioural change requires experimentation, persistence, training and, most of all, constructive feedback within a safe environment from trusted colleagues.

Change requires more than the encouraging and persuasive words of leaders. It requires active investment in people to build new capabilities that are sustainable and adaptable over time. Leaders must ask themselves what support they have provided to enable people to build these new skills and adopt the new behaviours required for success. More time must be committed to coaching, with positive reinforcement of strong will, even if the skill isn't yet evident. Research by Phillipa Lally et al in 2009 concluded that consistently adopting new behaviours takes sixty-six days of persistence and coaching.[20] That's a lot of trial, error and determination, but after two months, behavioural change can be successfully embedded. Ask any leader of failed culture change if sixty-six days is a long time to wait and most would say, with hindsight, 'No time at all.'

The responsibility for capability development is obviously two-way. The individual and the company need to invest time and energy into pursuing this goal for mutual benefit. For successful adoption of new behaviour to occur, the company must develop training assets and adjust relevant processes. Leaders are obliged to set an example of 'learning' to their teams and commit time to coaching. This all sounds obvious, but the percentage of leaders who do

---

20 P Lally, CHM van Jaarsveld, HWW Potts and J Wardle, 'How are habits formed: Modelling habit formation in the real world', *European Journal of Social Psychology*, 40/6 (2010), 998–1009, https://doi.org/10.1002/ejsp.674

There is no magic formula
for culture change.

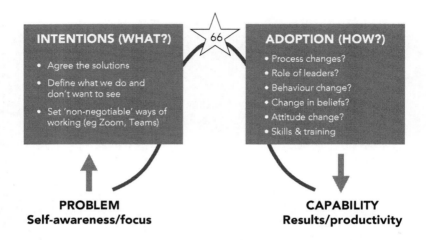

PROBLEM
Self-awareness/focus

CAPABILITY
Results/productivity

not commit adequate time to coaching their people is extremely high. In our experience, over 80% of leaders overestimate how much coaching they are providing,[21] and nearly all leaders struggle to provide coaching consistently across the team. Sufficient time dedicated to coaching is also the *lowest* scoring leadership trait in the entire Redpill database when reviewed in the context of 360-degree feedback given by reportees to their line managers. This could be due to managers overestimating their reportees' capabilities, or the unconscious bias we all carry connected to liking and disliking others, where we spend more time with those we 'like'. Further, it could be associated with high- and low-capability people, where we gravitate towards those with whom we feel most comfortable. This often neglects those we either don't connect with personally, or those whom we believe are already competent. We also tend to confuse 'task supervision and review' with 'coaching'. This is never black and white, but well-intended coaching time often gets substituted by urgent task management. The reality is, development and coaching of team members is often a neglected activity and something that should be tracked consciously to help

---

21 Redpill CompetenceQ database

form new habits, especially during periods of culture change.

When someone feels *unable* to perform a task, the prevailing culture will determine how it manifests in their behaviour. In a safe environment people will ask questions, seek insight and be open. In unsafe environments, it is unlikely an employee will be as open about areas of incompetence. Instead, they will probably question the need for the change, which can appear like a questionable *attitude* to an outside observer. The challenge is for leaders not to judge things at face value until explored. Each time you are about to conclude someone is resisting the change due to bad attitude, make sure they feel competent. Ask yourself if you have checked capability and offered coaching to close gaps. Ask yourself is it reasonable to expect that the other person *can do it*.

Do they care?

If the first two questions can be answered positively, in other words, the individual understands what is needed and why, and is able to display the behaviour or skill competently, then resistance is more likely to be caused by a lack of motivation.

This final question is absolutely critical to successful culture change. Considering the attitude of people must also include their influence and energy. As a leader, you must ensure you have clearly articulated why this change brings a benefit to them personally, even if this benefit is merely their ability to retain their job. They must be able to answer the question, 'What's in it for me?'

In our experience, the number of people with genuinely poor attitude is less than 20% of employees. Of these, less than half will be energised enough to be a negative influence on others. When we compare this to the assumptions made by managers,

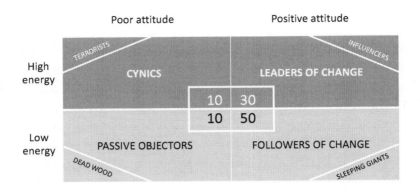

we observe that in over 45% of situations, the manager will explain the resistance as an employee's poor attitude or lack of motivation. This means that over 25% of your people may be being misjudged as lacking a positive attitude when another factor such as understanding or capability is the only thing stopping them from being positive about culture change. Part of this reality gap is a simple projection of 'blame', part is being disconnected from your team, and part may be legacy perceptions. The bottom line is that the judgement is often wrong.

We started this chapter by picturing the scene of a six-month-old culture change journey that was not delivering the required change. This is a typical timeframe for leadership patience to run out and can frequently be the moment culture change becomes a lower priority for the business. It is also roughly the time it takes a medium to large organisation to diagnose the situation, discuss the options and define future standards. At best, it's the end of the beginning or the 'defining the future' stage. It is certainly too early to be concluding that culture change has failed.

DIALOGUE

Purpose: To ask the team whether they are helping people succeed, or judging them unfairly.

Six months into a culture change journey is a good time to review early progress. Initiate a discussion focused on the 'Do they get it, can they do it, do they care?' model with the questions below:

- Did we communicate the change in a compelling and personal way? Do individuals understand the what, the why and the how of culture change?

- Are we providing the necessary time and resources to help our people change? Specifically, are we dedicating coaching time and providing training assets to support them?

- Do we have a small number of negative influences in the business? Do we need to replace them?

You may also include some people deeper in your organisation in this discussion to explore what may be missing for them.

Self-reflection

- Do I uncover the real reasons people are not changing, or do I judge them superficially?

- Have I made myself available to people who may benefit from my coaching them or mentoring them?

- Do I take action when people are genuinely disruptive and acting as a negative influence?

As leaders, we all need to learn to perform different roles in different teams.

16

To Team, Or Not To Team

I was reminded recently that the word 'team' is a common noun (person, place, or thing) and, therefore, 'static' by definition. Think about that for a minute. A 'team' is a static group of people. 'To team' (or 'teaming'), however, is a verb, and therefore active. Are teams static or active? Instead of talking about the characteristics of a team, maybe leaders should be talking about the more dynamic, active process of *teaming*. During culture change, the operative word is 'change', so leaders are facing an organisational environment that is adapting to the requirements to enable future success. This requires active thinking, a willingness to be constantly adapting and, critically, working with different people on different changes at different times. You may be on a sales team, a new product launch team and a culture change team all at the same time, sometimes on the same day. The word 'team' in organisations is increasingly less about 'my team' and more about *how I team*, but this is not how most people think of the word. As we've seen in a previous chapter, most of your energy as a manager or leader goes to those people that report to you (*my* team). Many people define their role in terms of the function they lead or the number of people they lead (static definitions). They need a mindset shift.

Teaming to learn

To team is about how we interact with others to achieve a goal (or more likely, goals). It is our ability to adopt a set of teaming principles and perform different team roles dependent on the situation. In one team we may be 'facilitator'; in another, 'expert'; in another, 'supporter', etc. In my experience, most managers and leaders seek to build a strong team rather than become a good teamer, but teaming is fundamentally about creating synergy and learning. We learn by asking questions of others that know something we don't, or can do something we can't. When people learn from each other, they create synergy by those same two people having knowledge and capability they previously didn't possess. Place this in a 'team' context and you have multiple opportunities for synergy and learning. Organisations that don't 'learn to team' or 'team to learn' will ultimately fail in the same way that some big corporate names have failed in the past twenty years. For example, and in my opinion:

- Blockbuster failed to adapt to video streaming.

- Kodak failed to adapt to digital photography.

- General Motors failed to adapt to empowering people.

- Nokia failed to adapt to the smartphone revolution.

- Toys R Us failed to adapt to e-commerce.

Teaming to learn is the fundamental belief that people can create synergy. In Chapter 1 (I Wonder...), we looked at the impact that curiosity can have on learning. Curiosity is also a critical part of successful teaming, but there's a lot more to teaming that just asking questions and being open-minded. Teaming fundamentally requires everyone to place the needs of the team above the needs of themselves. In other words, *giving* ahead of *receiving*: give my knowledge, give my support, give my feedback, give my challenge, give of my best in the role I have in this team… In return, we usually (if not always) receive similar gifts from others. Receiving sounds easier, right? Wrong. Receiving is often less easy to do. How well do leaders you know generally receive support and challenge? The competencies required to team successfully must be both given and received. Dependent on the team or the situation, there may be an emphasis on one or the other.

Teaming requires psychological safety

Teaming also depends on psychological safety (see Chapter 7: Safe Is Not Soft) and this is the role of leaders in the teaming process. Providing the safety to experiment, fail, learn, contribute and challenge is fundamental to *teaming*. If leaders see themselves as boss, supervisor and progress-chaser, they will organise check-ins, one-to-one reviews and update meetings. All of these will require the people coming to 'our' meeting and preparing their updates for 'us'. The updates will probably consist of PowerPoint slides explaining that the subordinate is doing a good job and that any issues are being resolved. All possible questions will hopefully be anticipated. The message will be optimistic, as 'supervisors' rarely receive bad news well. This process is time-consuming, distracts people from meaningful work and usually achieves precisely nothing. The subordinate often leaves the meeting having provided an update on the mundane, but not having addressed the real issues affecting the performance of their team. The deck is binned and they get back to work.

If leaders see themselves as 'on the team', they get involved and stay close to their team-mates, hear about the issues and help resolve them, and add value and create synergy rather than distract others and waste their time. Teamer leaders don't preside over the team, they're active within the team. Of course, there may be some decisions that have to be made, but those decisions become much easier with open and transparent ongoing communication, rather than staged, over-prepared reviews. Being a good teamer is why leadership in progressive cultures is much more challenging than leadership in hierarchical/traditional cultures. Teaming requires leaders to accept different roles in different teams rather than the homogenous 'supervisory' role performed in hierarchies, so adaptability and humility become necessary skills. Ask yourself:

- Am I able to perform a team role as organiser, another as supporter, and another as subject matter expert, and see all of these as part of my 'leadership role'?

- Do I have the humility, vulnerability and self-awareness to see the need for my role to adapt, or do I always play the role of supervisor, director and (pseudo) expert?

- In which direction do I think my teams need me to move?

Culture change is, by definition (at an organisational level), inclusive. As a senior leader, you will be part of a team leading the change. You will be the leader of the team adapting to the change. You may have interactions with stakeholders (internal and external) beyond the organisation in question who are not exposed to the change and whose expectations also need to be managed. Your team role is complex and your ability to adapt your teaming behaviours to different situations will be important for success. As businesses become more complex, more matrix and more global, we will need to be good 'teamers' rather than just good team leaders.

 **DIALOGUE**

Purpose: To introduce the concept of 'teaming' and recognise that it is a multifaceted capability.

Facilitate a discussion about 'team' and 'teaming'. The questions below may help you:

- What do we regard as our primary team? (The team I lead, my peer group, the whole business.)

- Do we encourage our senior leaders to see themselves as part of several teams?

- Do we display a safe team environment by the way we interact with each other?

- What parts of our business could be more effective if the concept of 'teaming' was introduced?

Self-reflection

Ask yourself the questions below. With which ones are you least satisfied with your own answer? Ask each member of your team this same question over the next week or two:

1. Do I care about the team I'm *in* (peers) as much as the team I *lead* (subordinates)?

2. What different 'team' roles do I perform? Do I recognise this difference in my approach and behaviour in each of them?

3. What teams could I add value to where I currently don't have a role?

Basically most business cultures are masculine, and to succeed in the future they will need to be more balanced.

17

The Feminine Touch

I am a fifty-nine-year-old white male (he/him/his). I grew up in England in the 1960s and 70s. I went to an all-boys school until sixth form, when ten unfortunate girls joined a group of 120 boys as an 'experiment'. I'm sporty and I've always felt included, I have never struggled with my weight, and I'm over 6 feet tall. I have had a pretty comfortable life. That makes me possibly one of the most privileged people on the planet. It's also why I try extremely hard not to behave like one. I purposefully try to learn from others, especially those that will be brutally honest with me. I read books addressing the major inequalities in our society, but I recognise that I will never be female, gay or black, for example, and must never be complacent and think I can truly empathise.

Organisations that don't consider diversity, equality and inclusion while managing culture change are sure to fail so I decided to ask two women for their perspective of what organisations should be mindful of when trying to change their culture. This chapter was initially intended to be written as their two interviews: Maria, who has twenty-five years' experience as an HR leader (including over ten years' experience of helping organisations with culture change), and Emily, my Millennial daughter who recently completed a psychology degree at the University of Manchester before embarking on a teaching career. Emily immediately advised me not to interview two white females and introduced me to her friend. Karla is a black, Danish national living and working in the UK. As you will discover, this was not the last change to my plan.

Interview 1: Maria's perspective

Kevin: Maria, you've held senior positions in business for the past twenty years. What quality do you think has helped you most?

Maria: *Pause.* I think I'm rational. I'm able to think both rationally and emotionally and I think this has helped me succeed in a man's world.

Kevin: A man's world?

Maria: Of course, it's a man's world. I remember my first management board position. I was an HR director. That was pretty much the only senior role available to women in the early 2000s. Gender stereotyping was (maybe still is) common in Poland and HR was usually the only female presence at a senior level. It's an indicator of a masculine culture when roles are assigned by gender relevance. Lorry drivers are men, nurses are women, engineers are men, HR directors are women. It's ridiculous and a consequence of masculine values. In Scandinavia, a feminine society, this gender role designation is much less prevalent.

Kevin: I agree, and I want to come back to this point later, but please tell me about the 'rational' comment you made about yourself.

Maria: In my experience, and I don't want to overgeneralise, men are rational beings. They look for competence and logic and functional expertise. In my first senior role, I gained credibility because I was able to demonstrate technical competence and engage in debates that were fact-based, rational discussions. I used facts, numbers, trends, rankings and business cases. This allowed me to be part of *the club*. Well, it at least allowed me into the club. I believe I'm more rational than many women and this gave me an advantage. I survived because I was a bit like the guys.

Kevin: The club?

Maria: The boy's club. They exist everywhere. Culturally, as a senior woman executive, you either choose to adapt to this reality, or feel a bit of an outsider. I managed to win over my male colleagues by being a bit like them and only then could I really influence the conversation. Even then I felt lonely. I had a sense that I was bringing topics to the table that were not supported publicly, but often supported privately after the event. It felt like associating with a more 'feminine' perspective was risky for my male colleagues, but they often privately let me know they agreed. By having a rational credibility, I was able to introduce more emotional themes gradually, and this is where I believe I really added value. A less rational woman would have a much tougher task. So, I eventually won them over by talking *their* language, which to some extent was also quite natural for me. Only then was I able to slowly introduce more balanced themes to the agenda.

Kevin: It sounds as though the challenge for your male colleagues was moving from passive public behaviour to active public behaviour?

Maria: Exactly. They didn't disagree with me in public forums, they simply left me fighting alone with my ideas, because by agreeing, they risked being perceived as too soft by others. I think this is what created the loneliness. The bigger the group, the less likely I was to receive public support and the more exposed I was. There was one occasion where we had to lay people off. Many of those affected were approaching retirement and would probably not find new jobs in Communist Poland. I suggested we conduct some training to help us handle these difficult conversations. The idea was rejected, but later resurrected with me privately when the trauma of these discussions proved too much for some board members.

Kevin: In your experience as a consultant, do you believe this stereotyping has changed?

Maria: It varies massively by organisation. I truly believe the current younger generation are thinking about gender balance and culture balance differently. They come to the topic without prejudice or assumptions. It's refreshing and gives me hope for the future. Where you have a group of homogenous men of a certain age running businesses, not much is changing, in my experience.

Kevin: Surely diversity is on everyone's agenda?

Maria: Yes and no. It's on the agenda, but motives vary significantly. At one end of the spectrum, you have the 'reluctant metric' approach. Masculine businesses love metrics. These are organisations chasing numerical gender balance, often because of societal pressure. They'll set a target for all sorts of measurable change. This isn't real. It's fake, and probably won't help in the long term. A tick-box exercise, if you like. Many of the women who succeed are like I was in 2001. They're able to adapt to a man's world. Some adapt their appearance; some adapt their approach. There's plenty of research that says if you have *gender balance* in teams for the sake of it, you'll probably not achieve any improvement in performance. At the other end of the spectrum, if you have a *culturally balanced* approach where you seek a balance of beliefs, whether held by men or women, you are creating the environment for true diversity of thinking.

Kevin: Are you saying that pursuit of gender balance is a waste of time?

Maria: No, I'm saying culture balance is arguably more important and more likely to deliver the cultural objectives sought, which are usually themes like empathy, care, support and people-centricity. These counterbalance themes like performance, metrics, conflict and reason. As we both know, a typical man in a feminine culture such as Sweden will show more care and empathy than a typical woman in a competitive culture such as the USA.

Kevin: So, when do we know that an organisation has it right?

Maria: When the culture of the organisation reflects the business need. This will usually require balanced cultural perspectives with a moderate bias to certain cultural poles, as needed. This might be more masculinity, or more femininity. As soon as you have extreme cultural beliefs driving decision-making, you will underperform, in my view. An all-male, all-masculine team or an all-female, all-feminine team will often fail. Female gender is not synonymous with feminine culture. Nor is male gender synonymous with masculine culture. A mix of gender and a mix of feminine/masculine cultural beliefs is best, with cultural values not recognised as a proxy for gender. Basically, most cultures are masculine and to succeed in the future they will need to be more balanced.

Kevin: I really like this perspective. You don't necessarily increase emotional intelligence by recruiting female leaders; rather, you need people of any gender who hold feminine cultural beliefs. This isn't the perspective of many organisations, who mostly chase diversity metrics.

Maria: Exactly, if the motive is culture change towards more feminine values, then recruiting more women probably won't work by itself. If the motive is to reflect society, then gender balance is important, but I'm not sure that culture change is then the motive.

Kevin: So, I might not get a feminine perspective for this book by talking to two females?

Maria: You might not. I suggest you talk to a couple of people, men or women, with strong feminine values.

This lightbulb moment occurred in real time. My interview with Maria had just demonstrated that I had fallen into the same trap as virtually everyone else. I thought I'd get a feminine cultural perspective by talking to two females. I'm sharing this insight because it's so easy to make this mistake, even if you're a so-called 'expert'. I decided to contact an old friend and colleague from Coors Brewers, Tara, who is a good example of someone who holds feminine values. Tara is now an executive and team coach with over sixteen years' experience in this field. When I first knew her, Tara was a senior executive and had resigned from Coors when I was her line manager in 2005. I was curious about her reasons and motives. With some trepidation, I asked her for an interview and she agreed within an hour.

Interview 2: Tara's perspective

Kevin: Tara, I'm so grateful to you for agreeing to do this interview. I have to say, I'm a bit nervous.

Tara: *Laughs.*

Kevin: In my previous interview with Maria, she suggested that feminine values are more important than female gender equality. Would you agree with that statement?

Tara: It depends what you're trying to achieve. If you're trying to improve the diversity of thinking in your organisation, then I think gender diversity, or any diversity, will help create that. If you're attempting to drive culture change towards a more feminine culture, then having women on the board is not necessarily going to achieve that.

Kevin: So, you're both agreed on that point. My interview with Maria also brought me to the conclusion that feminine values in business are critical to achieving cultural balance. I've always seen you as someone who holds feminine values, so I'm curious about how you've felt when you've been working in masculine cultures.

Tara: Well, I was always trying to be one of the boys, because I thought I had to adapt to fit in. I distinctly remember a 'personality type' discussion with you and your senior team at Coors. I was a 'yellow/green' type and you were all 'red/blue' types. I was saying, 'But I'm not like you,' and you said, 'We don't want you to be like us, we want you to be you.' I'd spent my whole career trying to fit in, but because I hold feminine values, it had become exhausting for me. Driving for success and going for sales cost me a lot. After I left the business, I spent the next year 'unpicking myself' and peeling back the onion, removing the masks to find who I really was. It wasn't this pseudo-sales leader that I pretended to be. I imagine there are still a lot of women doing this, still adapting and paying the price. The leadership competencies that are valued most highly in organisations are still very masculine.

Kevin: This is what I wanted to discuss. It's quite well established that the leadership traits you need to change culture are feminine leadership traits such as care, support and empathy. These are the traits that enable adaptation, trust and closer relationships. In our consulting work, we have much more success helping feminine cultures become a bit more masculine than masculine cultures become a bit more feminine, and of course, what you're looking for is this balance. Have you ever found this balance in your work?

Tara: That's a really interesting question. In the worlds I operate in, I'd have to say no. I've observed that teams with more introverts often have a softer approach, but I'm not sure feminine cultural values are lived in many organisations. One of my clients does have 'care' as a value.

Kevin: 'Care' is an interesting value. We often see this, and other feminine values, being less well lived than the masculine values. They're almost there only because leaders think they should be, not because leaders believe it will help the organisation improve or succeed.

Tara: Take the NHS in the UK, for example. Clearly, the NHS wants to provide care to its patients, but internally, it's hierarchical, metric-driven and very masculine.

Kevin: Can an organisation be *caring* externally if it doesn't hold a value of *care* internally?

Tara: Can a business embrace feminine values if it's dominated by metrics? No. One of the things I espouse is compassionate leadership – male, female or non-binary – it doesn't matter, any gender can be compassionate by espousing forgiveness, tolerance and patience, for example. These are the qualities that really engage people, especially in situations of change, and ultimately drive performance.

Kevin: Changing tack a little, can you tell me about your role on the board of 'Women in Banking & Finance'?

Tara: Sure. This is a volunteer organisation that's trying to influence positive change in the industry. They do a lot of research and run events to support local members. We run sessions on things like building self-confidence. I guess we're helping them by giving the right support to enable them to thrive in a masculine world, which banking still is. In essence, we help them play the game until they reach a level of genuine influence, without losing sight of who they are like I did. We need to do this at a middle-management level rather than at a non-executive director level (which, unfortunately, was the way the UK has historically legislated). More women on non-executive boards is an easy headline rather than a genuine force for changing organisations. A group of men probably came up with this idea.

Kevin: If you think about leadership work, this will often be linked to culture change. You said earlier that diversity isn't pursued simply for culture change, so what do you find is the most important driver of culture change?

Tara: It's always the values. It starts here and may be supported by diversity. If you have the right values and you live them, you will attract a more diverse population of employees. I've always said, 'Don't fix the women, fix the culture.'

Kevin: So, how do a group of men truly embrace feminine values?

Tara: They need a compelling 'why'. *Why* do they believe a more feminine culture will help the business succeed? If they can't answer this question, they won't change. If they believe that caring for their people will result in their people giving 100%, they will drive care and not numbers.

Kevin: This is fascinating. We all need to spend a lot more time at the early stages of culture change when beliefs and values are being created, making sure they're genuine beliefs and not simply throwaway statements of political correctness. There's always a temptation to define this stage far too quickly without thinking of consequences. Thank you so much for your thoughts, Tara.

So far, two women I have a huge amount of respect for had both told me gender diversity won't necessarily create a feminine culture and both had talked about having to adapt to fit in. In Maria's case, it was easier because she was a rational type; for Tara, it was exhausting because she is more emotionally motivated. I wondered how many people like Tara organisations lose because they fail to embrace who they really are. Both Maria and Tara also agreed that once you have a degree of credibility, more feminine agendas can be driven. Finally, both agreed that introducing a feminine balance to most current (masculine) cultures is critical. I had one niggle. I still didn't quite understand how gender balance and cultural balance worked together as two positive forces, but I had a hypothesis. I needed to check my thinking with Maria again.

Kevin: Maria, I need to dig a bit deeper on the gender vs culture question. Specifically, when we have the cultural balance defined as part of our genuine beliefs and we need to implement this change in everything we do, is this when gender diversity becomes more critical?

Maria: *Pause.* I think this could be true. When we've defined the culture change required to help the business become more successful, we then start to *embed* the change. In my opinion, this is why we need gender diversity and, frankly, every diversity. White will never experience black, male will never experience female, able-bodied will never experience disabled. When we make changes in organisations, we need the balanced *experience* of everyone to help us design the solution. Women have experiences men will never have, nor fully understand and vice versa. Creating a culture is different to defining a culture.

My final interview with Karla had a slightly different motive. Both Tara and Maria were successful women leaders who started their careers in the 1990s. What would a black, Danish Millennial working in the UK have to say on the topic?

Interview 3: Karla's perspective

Kevin: Karla, thank you so much for agreeing to this interview. Maybe I could start by asking you to give me a quick summary of who you are, where you're from and how you found yourself in Manchester?

Karla: Well, I'm 27, a black woman, a Danish national, an ex-elite athlete and coach. I've lived and studied in Australia and worked in the Netherlands before coming to the UK eighteen months ago. I've worked in various jobs in Denmark, for a major sports brand in the Netherlands and now a sports retailer in the UK.

Kevin: Karla, you put me to shame. I'd hardly ventured beyond Yorkshire by twenty-seven! So, given your experience, when you hear the words 'work culture', what do you think of?

Karla: Work–life balance. It's the biggest difference I notice between working in Denmark or the Netherlands compared to the UK. In Denmark, work is only part of your life. In the UK, it seems to be everything. The irony is, I give a lot more of myself to my company when they recognise that I have a life beyond work.

Kevin: You're saying you actually work harder when the company makes a point of encouraging you to keep a balance?

Karla: Yes, without doubt. My company in the Netherlands had me 100% from day one. In the high-pressure environment of the UK, I'm up and down.

Kevin: What are the main reasons for this?

Karla: Lack of trust and focus on relationship-building.

Kevin: Both feminine cultural characteristics.

Karla: Yes, I suppose they are, and they're characteristics that prioritise relationships and allow people to have fun at work. It sounds obvious, but I don't experience it as much in the UK. In Denmark and the Netherlands, we would just have a drink together from time to time and get to know each other. It helped me understand the people I was working with and trust them. Ultimately, it felt safer and helped us work together more effectively. I want to know the people I work with and understand them. Then I can empathise and support them.

Kevin: What is your perspective of UK work culture?

Karla: It's all about how you show up. Long hours, deliver results, hit targets.

Kevin: Masculine cultural characteristics. So, how do you feel in UK work culture?

Karla: A bit of an outsider. The 'lads' have their jargon, which sometimes I don't understand. I feel like I'm always trying to adapt and never quite achieving it. I think the biggest influence on how I feel is my manager. In the Netherlands, my manager was empathic and aware of my needs. They acted as a buffer between the demands of American owners and the needs of their team.
Here in the UK, not so much, so you feel the top-down pressure more. It's also more apparent in the UK that peer groups don't really support each other for the good of the company. They tend to compete more with each other, so the competitive edge is internal rather than external, which is ironic, because that's where the real competitor is.

Kevin: Again, you're describing 'competitive' masculine culture. These cultures often claim to be market-focused, but are wasting an enormous amount of energy competing with each other internally. Did the relationships in Denmark and the Netherlands have other benefits?

Karla: Well, in Denmark I think communication is more honest. More direct. Yes, communication is more effective. Relationship-building was also seen as *part of the job*. Time was actually allocated to the relationship-building. My manager would encourage me to go for a coffee with key people in other functions, because she believed we would collaborate better if we knew each other.

Kevin: Tell me about how teamwork felt in your different experiences.

Karla: I found teams, and leaders of teams, shared more in both the Netherlands and Denmark than they do in the UK. We had a lot more structure to make sure everyone was aligned. If my manager found a way to do something efficiently and effectively, she would share that with her peers. Here in the UK, team leaders seem to send their own message to their teams, and often that message can differ enormously. They don't seem to align as much. We don't share processes and we don't share effective ways of working, which I find really strange. It's not good for the business and it's harder for people to move around.

Kevin: It sounds as though they compete more.

Karla: Yes, until you mentioned it just now, I hadn't thought of it that way before, but that's exactly what they do. We don't talk about helping each other, it's more sink or swim. And nothing's ever good enough. Even when I know I've done a good job, it doesn't feel like it.

Kevin: If you could have ten minutes with the managing director of your current business, what one thing would you say to them that would help the business be more successful?

Karla: Education. Education about differences and building empathy with our diverse customers and with each other.

Bingo.

The interview with Karla is, of course, an interview with one person and cannot be taken as a proxy for everyone's experience in any of the countries she mentioned. Masculine and feminine work cultures will exist, to varying degrees, in every country. However, forgetting the countries for a minute, the *culture types* were so clearly articulated, it provided another personal lightbulb moment for me. As people and businesses the world over adapt to changes in working methods, and employees have more choices available to them regarding where they live, how they live and are driven by more than just financial rewards, it was becoming increasingly clear to me that more feminine, and less masculine, cultures are more likely to adapt and enable culture change. Feminine cultures are more empathic, more supportive and more compassionate. These, plus other characteristics, are often the missing links in organisations pursuing change. These adaptive cultures will attract a diverse workforce and ultimately be more successful and rewarding places to be. After twelve years of non-judgemental observation of organisational culture, I was realising that some feminine cultural characteristics were almost certainly a necessary pre-condition for successful change, including the genuine pursuit of diversity. Diversity driven by masculine metrics was doomed to be a top-down tick-box exercise. Diversity driven by a genuine desire for care, people and relationships seemed to have more chance of success. I decided to make this the topic of my second book, and the concept of *The Feminine Touch* was born.

 **DIALOGUE**

Purpose: To discuss whether your team are pursuing diversity for the right reasons. To align on understanding the difference between gender diversity benefits and feminine cultural benefits.

- What are we aiming to achieve by driving diversity?

- Is our culture too masculine? (See Chapter 4: Culture Enables Strategy.)

- Do we need to drive gender diversity and feminine cultural beliefs?

Self-reflection

- Do I confuse the assumed benefits of gender diversity with balancing feminine and masculine culture traits?

- Do I create the space for my team(s) to develop constructive relationships with others?

- Do I observe team members trying to fit in rather than being their authentic selves?

A leader's response to bad news is a litmus test for healthy culture.

18

Sh!t Happens

Not much is certain in life, but one truth you can bank on when it comes to culture change is that it will not be easy. You will face significant headwinds, distractions and resistance. Perhaps the most common issue faced by culture change champions is when business performance fails to meet expectations. This is a double challenge during culture change. On the one hand, does your culture *enable you to cope with bad news?* And on the other, does culture change stay in focus *as a priority* when the business is missing its financial goals?

A leader's response to bad news is a litmus test

If you work for a leader who prefers fake good news to reality-checked bad news then you may feel increasingly frustrated by inflated forecasts being missed, innovation projects being accelerated to gap-fill the P&L and feeling personally unable or unsafe to speak truthfully about the issues and problems that exist in the business. How leaders respond to bad news defines the safety that exists in your organisation and forms the basis on which learning does or doesn't happen. For the past two years, I have run more than 200 psychological safety surveys with teams in more than forty organisations. Below are the two statements that score lowest across our entire database:

1. I am able to openly say what needs to be said, even if it's bad news, without any fear of negative consequences.

2. Failure and making mistakes are always seen as an opportunity to learn.

It is deeply ironic, yet often the case, that middle managers have a better grasp of business issues than management boards. In my experience, the main reason for this is the way these senior leaders react and respond to bad news and problems. One leader in a client organisation recently said to his team, 'Don't bring me problems. Bring me solutions!' This is a classic superficial statement and the inevitable consequence is that he will only get to hear about the problems that have already been solved, so he is redundant in the problem-solving process. He's not involved in either the solved, or unsolved, problems. The intention and motive of this leader is to encourage his team to take responsibility for the problem and try to solve it. This is a positive intention, but it must also be safe for the team to bring *unsolved* problems to the table, or they remain unsolved. Ultimately these 'good news' leaders may see the consequence of these hidden problems, but often when it is too late and the business suffers. The higher up this attitude is demonstrated within an organisation, the less connected leaders become within the business and the more the business relies on middle managers to solve problems. This is compounded by culture typology. In egalitarian cultures where a combination of 'closer' boss relationships and 'independence' prevails, you may get some issues being raised with the 'bring me solutions' leader because the force of expressing one's opinion is strong enough.

In all forms of hierarchy, forget it. Even before these words were spoken, the likelihood of issues being raised was low. Now it's zero.

The reality is that over 90% of the companies we have surveyed in the past ten years are organised as hierarchies of some sort. Leaders need to be mindful of the positively intended soundbites they throw out to their teams and they need self-discipline when the bad news does come.

I mentioned earlier that your *reaction* to bad news is a good test of your culture's health. Let's assume a leader has not asked only for solutions and is open to a few snippets of bad news and the odd unsolved problem. What is their reaction when the bad news presents itself? This is a complex issue dependent on where the issue emerges from and how effectively expectations are managed. Fortunately (or unfortunately), and dependent on your position in the pecking order, *issues* tend to be communicated up the line and *expectations* are communicated down the line. This is a major problem.

Let's consider a three-year planning process where the top-down growth target is 7% and the market is flat. Everybody knows this is an unrealistic stretch, but the innovation pipeline has generated high expectations and top-down leaders sound confident. As we cascade this target into the business with some targets slightly higher and some slightly lower than the generic 7%, the sense of frustration is real. After the first quarter the business is predictably flat, but leaders stick with the target. The growth requirement for the rest of the year is now compounded and close to 10%. Innovation projects are accelerated to fill some of the gap, subsequently rushed to market. Inevitably, some fail. Organic growth requirement is now close to 15%. Our leaders do not like bad news, so they didn't *hear* the messages that the market is flat, innovation needs time to develop and test, and competitors are also becoming more aggressive to protect share. The issue didn't translate up the line and the top-down expectations weren't up for debate by the time they landed in the sales office. Maybe I exaggerate, business is much more sophisticated than this, but I have seen it too many times in both my career in business and in consulting to ignore this common reality.

There's more bad news. The sales team are now chasing the numbers. Our 'good news' leader will be asking for 'solutions'. This means commercial compromises will be made, margin will be sacrificed (sometimes forever) and portfolio balance will be forfeited for the product that might be able to fill the gap. Usually, this is a big volume product where the long-term margin erosion is highest and market position is strongest, meaning we focus less time and energy on the strategic growth areas like innovation. We're now in a downward spiral of bad decisions, tactical short-termism and frustration.

Dependent on where we sit in the organisation, we will sense and feel this differently. The most senior managers will be confused, because there is no line of sight to the problem and yet disappointing numbers. They're thinking, 'Maybe we need to change some personnel?' The directors running the show in market will not want to disappoint their bosses to whom commitments have been made, and so they place more pressures on middle managers and team leaders to make up the gaps, turning a blind eye to the problems. They're thinking, 'I need to hit the number and worry about "strategy" next year.' The managers at the operational end of the business are stressed by problems and issues communicated from their teams and pressure from above to hit the numbers. They're thinking, 'Why doesn't my boss listen?' The team at the customer interface are incredulous. They are forced to compromise on strategic priorities, margin and innovation, and take the quick wins available to them (which usually means dropping the price of the easiest product to sell up). All of this makes this year's plan more tactical and short-term, and next year's plan almost impossible. They're thinking, 'This isn't sustainable.'

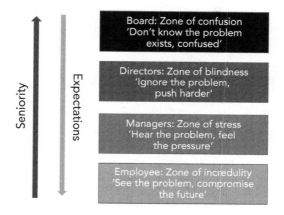

How does this cycle of disappointment get solved?

1. Ensure a safe environment exists for open and honest communication and interpersonal interaction (see Chapter 7: Safe Is Not Soft).

2. Invest in market data that removes the emotion from contextualising why targets and expectations are unrealistic.

3. Make it clear to your team that you need to hear the bad as well as the good news – as Jim Collins described it in his 2001 book, *Good to Great*, 'the *brutal facts*'.[22]

---

22 JC Collins, *Good to Great: Why some companies make the leap... and others don't* (Random House Business, 2001)

4. Learn not to react defensively or with disappointment towards the individual that's delivering the honest bad news.

5. Carve out time in the agenda to focus on the learning that emerges from the bad news.

6. Be brave and use the bad news as a lever.

Using bad news as a lever is powerful

In 2009, I was faced with a dilemma. I was Commercial Director for the biggest brewer in Poland. We enjoyed a commanding 41% market share and had grown share every year for the past three years. Our biggest competitor had a 34% share. A big gap. Our strategy was to grow share with the mainstream and premium retailers and broaden our portfolio offer with premium international brands and innovation. The usual stuff. We did not trade with 'discount retailers' (our description, not theirs) or supply them with private label products. The CEO was adamant it should remain that way to protect brand equity and value. One day at a strategy review, I presented a brutal fact. So-called 'discounters' were growing so quickly that to retain our number one position in five years' time, we would need over 50% of the remaining market. This was highly unlikely, but even if somehow achieved, neither profitable nor sustainable. Our choice was to trade with discounters or be number two in 2014. The CEO stared me out for what felt like ten minutes and then said, 'Do what you have to do, but don't lose the number one position.' I had the market facts, I wasn't advocating one way or the other, simply offering a choice and testing the strategic intent. I presented this option dispassionately and outlined the consequences of various decisions. We consequently traded with what they now call 'convenience retail' and our number one position was protected and consolidated. None of the feared consequences previously stopping us trading with 'discounters' ever materialised.

Why was this discussion even possible? Because it was safe, or rather, I felt safe. I was also working for a company happy to invest in market data, prepared to consider challenges to long-held positions and willing to listen to some brutal facts. The CEO was a pragmatist whose decisions were informed by facts and data rather than opinion and emotion.

 **DIALOGUE**

Purpose: To get the brutal facts out on the table before they derail culture change.

Facilitate a discussion about what you talk about openly as a team. Create a list of what remains unsaid. What 'brutal fact' discussions need to be held? Gather these inputs without judgement or pushback. Then use a simple voting process to agree on topics for deeper discussion using this structure:

- Frame and define the topic in no more than two sentences. What is the unspoken issue?

- Why is it not discussed? Where does this barrier exist in the organisation?

- What possible solutions could be considered?

Usually, the second part of the second question is the sticking point, and for two completely different reasons. Sometimes, the barrier doesn't exist at all, except as a theoretical concept in people's minds based on a 'story' from ten years ago. Sometimes, the barrier is a person (or persons), usually senior, whose behaviour is the block. In this situation (by definition, unsafe), you need to find a way to make this senior person aware that their behaviour is the reason certain changes are not happening. The message needs to be delivered by a credible source – either an influential colleague or an external coach or consultant. Often, this self-awareness is all that's required. Of course, it doesn't always work, but I have experienced positive outcomes in over 75% of such cases.

Self-reflection

Ask yourself the following questions. Which of your answers are you least satisfied with? You can also ask each member of your team these same questions over the next week or two:

- How do I react to bad news? Do I welcome the truth and focus on the problem, or leave people thinking I am blaming them?

- Do I encourage 'brutal facts' discussions or do I assume that if issues aren't raised, they don't exist?

- Do I ensure time is spent learning from mistakes, or do I simply ask people not to repeat them?

Review And Next Steps

As this book has attempted to demonstrate, culture change is not a linear process. It cannot be treated as a project. You can't start at Chapter 1, follow the book to Chapter 18 and draw a line under it. Culture change is messy and difficult, but ultimately rewarding. This 'review' chapter will summarise the purpose of each chapter and suggest circumstances when rereading may be helpful for you.

Part One: Preparing for Culture Change

Chapter 1: I Wonder...

Purpose: To provoke a sense of wonderment that helps you rediscover lost curiosity of differences and empathy for others' opinions.

When is this chapter useful?

- When the organisation or team is repeatedly making the same mistakes

- When a team is constantly agreeing with itself

- When tasks and problems are always approached in the same way and people are suggesting the same solutions

Chapter 2: The 'Culture' Word

Purpose: To encourage you to think deeply about culture based on beliefs rather than outcomes or superficial headlines.

When is this chapter useful?

- When culture is being described in terms of desired outcomes, for example, winning culture, performance culture, blame culture or innovation culture, etc.

- When leadership teams are unable to clearly describe the 'beliefs' that underpin their desired outcomes

- When leaders are using the same words, for example, empowerment or challenge, but displaying different behaviours

Chapter 3: Data, Data, Data

Purpose: To create a tangibility to our collective understanding of culture by providing a language and multidimensional approach based on research.

When is this chapter useful?

- When leaders are looking for a way to frame a discussion on culture

- When alignment is missing, and data-based insight is required

- When differences of beliefs within a team are difficult to explain

Chapter 4: Culture Enables Strategy

Purpose: To explain a detailed dimensional and typology approach to culture using the StrategyQ tool developed by Redpill Consulting.

When is this chapter useful?

- When you wish to gather structured opinions from employees in the organisation

- When you need to prioritise the agenda for culture change

- When you need to understand the true breadth of opinion in your organisation

Chapter 5: Take Off Your Glasses

Purpose: To build awareness that we all see culture through our own unique, but limited, lens.

When is this chapter useful?

- When the team need to listen to each other more effectively and/or suspend judgement

- When senior leaders need to understand the difference between the organisational needs and their personal preferences

- When leaders are being judgemental about others' cultural beliefs

Chapter 6: Yin And Yang

Purpose: To understand how both behaviours and ways of working must change 'together' in order for culture to develop positively.

When is this chapter useful?

- When culture change is being advocated by leaders, but internal mechanisms are not facilitating this change

- When behavioural change is dependent on changes to ways of working, and vice versa

- As a 'ways of working' sense-check when you are prematurely concluding that your people are resisting change

Chapter 7: Safe Is Not Soft

Purpose: To position psychological safety as a critical prerequisite of culture change and provide a model to evaluate it.

When is this chapter useful?

- When the required change is not happening, and you're not sure why

- When you sense your organisation is not learning from mistakes or addressing problems constructively

- When you sense a lack of humility in your leadership team

Chapter 8: Consequences

Purpose: To ensure leaders understand the consequences of embarking on culture change to themselves, their teams and individuals.

When is this chapter useful?

- When you sense leaders are treating culture change as a project and may not be considering their long-term role in leading it

- When you are worried culture change will be fearful for the people you wish to retain

- When leaders see the need for change in others, but not in themselves

Part Two: Implementing Culture Change

Chapter 9: Part-time Leader

Purpose: To position culture as one of the most important *ongoing* leadership considerations.

When is this chapter useful?

- When leaders say they are too busy to focus on culture

- When leaders are over-delegating the management and leadership of culture change

- When the CEO or leader of your organisation does not accept and embrace the need for change in themself

Chapter 10: Tight/Loose

Purpose: To present a model of culture change that includes 'tight' items that must be consistently implemented and 'loose' elements that may have some local or functional nuances.

When is this chapter useful?

- When there are genuine contextual differences in parts of your business, for example, countries, business sectors or risk profiles

- When you have some leaders with valid personal concerns and need a methodology to engage them

- When your tight agenda requires significant changes in leadership behaviour

Chapter 11: Abracadabra

Purpose: To explain the futility of announcing culture change as the outcome of a project.

When is this chapter useful?

- When leaders are advocating announcing the 'results' of the culture change programme

- When some 'quick wins' are needed to send positive messages to the organisation

- When your business needs a new way to conduct 'meetings'

Chapter 12: Everyone, Or No One

Purpose: To stress the importance of culture being inclusive, with no one opting out.

When is this chapter useful?

- When an 'elite' group of people display behaviours that position them *above* everyone else

- When some people need to change at a different pace to others

- When peer group relationships are secondary to subordinate relationships

- When either advocacy or alignment is low among your leaders

Chapter 13: Energy Flow

Purpose: To show how the way we expend energy has a direct impact on the culture we build.

When is this chapter useful?

- When you have influential and independent leaders of function, but not much cross-functional cooperation

- When leaders see leading *their* team of direct reports as their primary role

Chapter 14: Pseudo-experts

Purpose: To encourage the reader not to mistake confidence for competence.

When is this chapter useful?

- When you sense that feminine/masculine cultural traits are out of balance

- When you sense that true expertise is not valued by senior leaders

- When you sense certain leaders are too set in their views about culture change

Chapter 15: Do They Get It? Can They Do It? Do They Care?

Purpose: To explain that there are a number of reasons why people don't change and to suggest a systematic self-appraisal before judging them.

When is this chapter useful?

- When leaders are jumping to the conclusion that bad attitude is the reason for people not changing

- When you are tolerating a small number of energetic cynics who are a negative influence on others

Chapter 16: To Team, Or Not To Team

Purpose: To suggest the traditional way of looking at the 'team' needs to be reframed so that people all see themselves as members of several teams (ie, 'teamers').

When is this chapter useful?

- When leaders find themselves performing different roles in different teams

- When part of culture change requires silos to be broken down

Chapter 17: The Feminine Touch

Purpose: To distinguish between feminine/masculine culture balance and female/male/non-binary gender balance.

When is this chapter useful?

- When the organisation is reflecting on its values and the masculine/feminine balance

- When the organisation is trying to shift towards a more feminine culture

- When the organisation seems to be pursuing diversity metrics for the wrong reasons

Chapter 18: Sh!t Happens

Purpose: To recognise that culture change, like any change, brings challenges (sometimes big ones) and mistakes are made. To illustrate that how we react to those mistakes determines whether they're made again.

When is this chapter useful?

- When leaders overly focus on the positive and avoid the negative

- When honesty is viewed as 'negative'

- When mistakes are made repeatedly

Over to you

If you want to use some of the tools mentioned in this book to begin your own team or company culture journey, please start by using the link below. This will take you to the Redpill StrategyQ survey. At the end of the survey, you can see a description of how you experience your organisational culture and how you believe it needs to change to support your strategic execution.

🌐 strategy.redpillconsulting.pl/ccc

It has been my intention to be constructive in my criticism and optimistic in my outlook. I passionately believe that cultural change can unlock working environments and help them become stimulating, exciting and fun places to be. Few cultures are beyond hope and most can be transformed with a relatively small number of changes. Leaders who pursue cultures that enable their strategic execution and inspire their teams to achieve their full potential are the leaders who will thrive in the future. It takes bravery, determination, resilience and time. It requires the maturity to think about the business beyond a leader's own tenure and the foresight to view their impact via a sustainable legacy of positive change rather than short-term financial metrics. These leaders are rare and special. Maybe you're one of them?

Acknowledgements

I have anonymously referred to several key influences in my career in this book, and this is probably the time to thank some of them. Of course, we all have many people to thank, but I will keep it to five individuals and groups, for five different reasons.

To my Kompania Piwowarska leadership team in 2008. Sorry for arriving with all the answers. I hope you are all thriving wherever you are.

To Peter Swinburn, for being the best boss I ever had, and my biggest learning influence, including my seminal moment at Newcastle airport in 1996.

To Maria Tykałowicz, for being my sounding board. I wish I had your brainpower and half your empathy, a rare combination.

To Magnus Alsterlind, for being the first leader to trust me with a culture project in 2012. I'm not sure you realised you were the first!

And finally:

To Greg Nicol, Geoff Fitzgerald and Neil Rodaway, my three best friends for forty years. Just thanks, guys.

The Author

Kevin Brownsey lives and works in Southern Portugal, regularly commuting to the UK and Poland, where he lived for fourteen years until 2021. Kevin spent the first twenty-four years of his career in a variety of commercial, HR and general management roles, mainly in the brewing industry.

For the past twelve years, he has run the organisational culture consulting business Redpill, working with large and small clients across Europe, the UK and the USA. He is the father of two children, Matthew and Emily, who live and work in Amsterdam and Manchester respectively. He regards giving his children an international education as the greatest gift he could offer them, to help them become tolerant world citizens.

He is passionate about sport and travels the world watching England and the British Lions rugby teams; he never misses a F1 Grand Prix; he is a die-hard Tottenham Hotspur fan and has recently developed an obsession with the racquet sport, padel. He is also a keen cyclist, runner and chess player.

In 2018, aged fifty-five, Kevin attempted to run a 250-km ultramarathon in the Namibian desert. He dropped out with salt deficiency and dehydration after 208 kms and considers coping with this failure as one of his greatest achievements.

🌐 strategy.redpillconsulting.pl/ccc

🌐 www.redpillconsulting.pl